Living Springs
Refreshing the Soul

JONATHAN Y.
MARTEY

WESTBOW·
PRESS
A DIVISION OF THOMAS NELSON
& ZONDERVAN

Scripture quotations, unless noted otherwise, are taken from the *Holy Bible,
New International Version®, NIV®*. Copyright 1973, 1978, 1984 by International
Bible Society. Used by permission of Zondervan. All rights reserved.

Scripture quotations marked "AMP" are taken from *The Amplified
Bible,* Old Testament. Copyright © 1965, 1987 by the Lockman
Foundation, Zondervan. Used by permission. All rights reserved.

Scripture verses marked "KJV" are from the King James Version of the Bible.

WestBow Press books may be ordered through booksellers or by contacting:

WestBow Press
A Division of Thomas Nelson & Zondervan
1663 Liberty Drive
Bloomington, IN 47403
www.westbowpress.com
1 (866) 928-1240

Because of the dynamic nature of the Internet, any web addresses or
links contained in this book may have changed since publication and may
no longer be valid. The views expressed in this work are solely those
of the author and do not necessarily reflect the views of the publisher,
and the publisher hereby disclaims any responsibility for them.

Any people depicted in stock imagery provided by Thinkstock are models,
and such images are being used for illustrative purposes only.
Certain stock imagery © Thinkstock.

ISBN: 978-1-4908-8012-9 (sc)
ISBN: 978-1-4908-8013-6 (hc)
ISBN: 978-1-4908-8011-2 (e)

Library of Congress Control Number: 2015907480

Print information available on the last page.

WestBow Press rev. date: 06/17/2015

Contents

DEDICATION

To the glory of God the Father, God the
Son, and God the Holy Spirit.
Also to Josephine, my precious wife, and our children,
Keren, Yehudi, Irene, Suzette, Titus, Uriel, and Iris.

FOREWORD

There is nothing as effective as the Word of God in bringing joy to the sorrowful, hope to the hopeless, healing to the sick, strength to the physically weak, comfort to the grieving, encouragement to the despairing, boldness to the meek, life to the dying, and the assurance of provision to the needy. Our Lord Jesus Himself outwitted Satan's temptation when He told him, "Man shall not live on bread alone but on every word that comes from the mouth of God" (Matthew 4:4). The Bible also tells us that "the Word of God is living and active and sharper than any two-edged sword" (Hebrews 4:12).

Living Springs Refreshing the Soul has come at a crucial time in the world today, when taking one's focus away from God and His immutable Word means being confronted with the fear and insecurity arising from global terrorism, disease, poverty, and natural and human-made disasters. It is truly a world that seems to be shaking anything and everything that can be shaken. No one seems immune to these global stirring-ups. In the midst of all these uncertainties, the only solid and steadying force or foundation one can truly depend on for stability and life's true meaning is the Word of God.

Through *Living Springs Refreshing the Soul,* Reverend Jonathan Martey has become a channel of God's blessings, assurance, comfort, and healing to an ailing world. The weekly pieces are truly inspirational. The way the author weaves together everyday life events and biblical truths and brings out their spiritual parallels is nothing short of inspired by the wisdom of God Himself.

I have personally been blessed by the *Inspirational Weekly* email messages of Reverend Martey which gave birth to this book. Each chapter of this fifty-two-week devotional speaks directly to the spirit and the soul of the reader, bringing the much-needed nourishment that only the Word of God can provide. The weekly devotionals, or chapters, of this book lead the reader in prayer and provide additional Bible resources for further reading and meditation during the week.

I trust and pray that as you read the weekly devotionals in *Living Springs Refreshing the Soul* and meditate on the Word of God, the Lord will meet your every need, be they physical, mental, emotional, social, financial, or spiritual. I also pray that those who are led to this book "by accident" will come to meet Christ in its pages and also become the beneficiaries of His unmerited grace and the gift of His salvation.

—Joyce Addo-Atuah, B. Pharm, MSc, PhD
Associate Professor, Touro College of Pharmacy, New York, NY, USA
Vice-President, Christ Coming Missionary Network, Hillside, NJ, USA
Past President, Aglow International, Gateway Chapter, Accra, Ghana.

Acknowledgements

When pregnancy reaches full term and the woman gives birth safely to a normal baby child, it brings joy to the woman, husband, family, and friends. There is great celebration and jubilation. The woman and her husband turn and show gratitude to some key individuals who stood with them during the period of pregnancy, labour, and delivery of the baby. So it is with the publication of *Living Springs Refreshing the Soul.* It's my turn to say thanks.

Glory be to God for inspiring the dream of a book that is intended to provide a basis for meditation on the Word of God and an impetus for exercising faith in God for daily victorious Christian living. In my exercising faith to write *Living Springs Refreshing the Soul,* God brought to me many comforters, motivators, and helpers. Key among them are the following people.

Josephine, my beautiful, sweet wife, tapped and rubbed my shoulders, providing prayers, tender loving care, and a sustained push to get this "baby" out. Her infectious faith opened doors of opportunities to connect to resources for the publication of *Living Springs Refreshing the Soul.* The pastors and congregation of Spirit and Word Church in Accra, Ghana, were like the mighty men of David. Each week of the past three years when I began preparing the write-up for *Living*

Springs Refreshing the Soul, they have surrounded me with an atmosphere of respect and held an appreciation of my life as a gift from God to them. That atmosphere provided the momentum to complete the book.

I shall forever be grateful for the voice of Professor Joyce Addo-Atuah of Touro College of Pharmacy, New York, USA, who, about two years ago, emailed me to encourage me to transform my weekly devotional materials into a book; this voice was echoed by Professor Alex Dodoo of the University of Ghana Medical and Dental School, in Accra, and Miss Margarita Apana of London. My unqualified gratitude goes to Rev. Dr. Philip Laryea of the Presbyterian Church of Ghana; Rev. Nii Clottey Odonkor of the Open Fountain Ministries in Tema, Ghana; and Professor Joyce Addo-Atuah, all of whom read through the first draft of the book and offered useful suggestions to make *Living Springs Refreshing the Soul* come to full term.

Last but not the least, my gratitude goes to my publisher, WestBow Press, for its "midwifery" role in bringing *Living Springs Refreshing the Soul* on to the scene.

INTRODUCTION

It was in mid-June 2011, eleven months after the painful loss of my wife, Pat, of blessed memory, when the Spirit of the Lord breathed into my soul the idea of a weekly devotional. I was then coming out of the depths of grief, moving to return to full circulation and move on in life. The purpose of the weekly devotional material, which I dubbed *Inspirational Weekly*, was, originally, to put within the reach of the congregation of Spirit and Word Church (SAWC) an inspiring, easy-to-read pamphlet for spiritual nourishment and victorious Christian living. Within three days of my hearing the Lord speak, the first volume of *Inspirational Weekly* was ready for distribution to the congregation of which I am the senior pastor. Ever since then, *Inspirational Weekly* has been churned out of the living wells of God's wisdom, with its weekly distribution reaching many people, by email, across Ghana, the United Kingdom, the United States, Canada, and beyond. Then came the prompting of the Spirit to get books published out of the volumes of *Inspirational Weekly*. These promptings were confirmed when some recipients of the *Inspirational Weekly*, notably Professor Joyce Addo-Atuah and Miss Margaret Apana, encouraged me to do so. This was the genesis of *Living Springs Refreshing the Soul*.

Once upon a time, the Lord Jesus stood by the well of Jacob in Samaria when a woman who had come to fetch water engaged Him in a conversation, as recorded in the Gospel according to Saint John, chapter four. Since they stood by a well, their conversation metamorphosed into aquatic matters and requests for water to drink. Water is life, and the only thing that quenches *thirst* is water. This *thirsty* Samaritan woman had come to get *natural* water, but Jesus ended up offering her *living* water. The Samaritan woman said to Jesus, "Sir, give me this water so that I won't get thirsty and have to keep coming here to draw water."

The chapters of *Living Springs Refreshing the Soul* have been drawn from deep *wells of inspiration* during my weekly "waitings" upon the Lord through prayer, worship, and the study of the Word of God. I have been amazed by God's sense of humour regarding the titles He proposed for the chapters of *Living Springs Refreshing the Soul* as well the contents of the chapters, which centre on everyday issues of life. Each chapter ends with a prayer and suggested Scripture quotations for further meditation. But I believe that the Holy Spirit will breathe upon souls each time the pages of *Living Springs Refreshing the Soul* are opened and read.

I trust that each chapter of *Living Springs Refreshing the Soul* will indeed reflect what the Lord said to the Samaritan woman: "Everyone who drinks this water will be thirsty again, but whoever drinks the water I give them will never thirst. Indeed, the water I give them will become in them a spring of water welling up to eternal life" (John 4:13–14 NIV).

—Jonathan Y. Martey

Chapter 1

The Springboard

Trust in the Lord with all your heart and lean not on
your own understanding; in all your ways submit to
him, and he will make your paths straight.

—Proverbs 3:5–6

New Year's Eve is annually marked with great gatherings in
places of worship and in popular squares in major cities and
many other parts of the world. There are spectacular displays
of fireworks in state capitals. From Accra to Zagreb, places
of worship, city squares, pubs, and nightclubs are filled with
people praying, singing, dancing, hugging, and kissing. For
the moment when the clock strikes midnight plus one second,
even people in war-torn countries burst into wild jubilations.
It is a cherished moment for many who participate in these
gatherings with the hope of better things in the New year to
come. Who welcomes whom? Is it the New Year that welcomes
the seven billion people living in the world, or is it, rather, the
seven billion people who welcome the New Year?

Soon, the excitement of a new year begins to fade away
with every tick of the clock. What has changed? Is it the date,

the time, the event, or the air we breathe? Whatever your answer may be, one thing is clear: another set of 365 days, of 52 weeks, of 12 months, is waiting to be explored. It is a path not travelled by any of us beginning on the first day of a new year. It is important, however, that we begin the journey from the right point of departure, a point I would like to call the *springboard*. For the purposes of our meditation in this chapter, let us define the word *springboard* as "a factor or an attitude that provides an opportunity for success." Anyone who stands on a springboard has an opportunity to gain height. And our best hope is to stand on the springboard of trust; I mean trust or confidence in the Lord God, who always takes the lead into each New Year.

Trust in God guarantees success; it enables one to gain height. Trust in God strengthens the cords of our tents in the midst of a storm. Trust in Him and in His promises. With the major economies of the world walking on tightropes and shaking in panic, there can be no safer or more stable ground than relying on the help that comes from God. Hear what the prophet Jeremiah says in Jeremiah 17:7–8: "Blessed is the man who trusts in the Lord, and whose hope is the Lord. For he shall be like a tree planted by the waters, which spreads out its roots by the river, And will not fear when heat comes; But its leaf will be green, and will not be anxious in the year of drought, nor will cease from yielding fruit." This is the time to pile up confidence in God. As when a plane is ready to take off and the aerodynamics of the engine are put in take-off mode, our trust must be in God, who has taken the lead into the year and has made provision for the fuel needed for the long-haul flight throughout the year.

God gives us reasons why He goes ahead of us into the year: "I will go before thee and make the crooked places straight; I will break in pieces the gates of brass, and cut in sunder the bars of iron" (Isaiah 45:2). You and I can cheer up, knowing that God has taken His stand as far as the challenges of every year are concerned. Therefore, jump onto the springboard of trust. You will bounce over and above every situation that seeks to contradict your expectations for the year. Some people trust in chariots and some in horses, but we will remember the name of the Lord our God. God says He watches over His Word to fulfil it, so let's get the following promises of God into our spirits to spur us on to victory. In Hebrews 13:5b, God says, "I will never leave you, never will I forsake you"; in Jeremiah 30:17, God says, "But I will restore to you health and heal your wounds"; in Jeremiah 31:16, God says, "Restrain your voice from weeping and your eyes from tears, for your work will be rewarded"; in Isaiah 65:22–24, God speaks volumes of what He will do for all who are called by His name—and this includes you and me.

> No longer will they build houses and others live in them, or plant and others eat. For as the days of a tree, so will be the days of my people; my chosen ones will long enjoy the works of their hands. They will not toil in vain or bear children doomed to misfortune; for they will be a people blessed by the Lord, they and their descendants with them. Before they call I will answer; whilst they are still speaking I will hear.

What do you believe God for in this year? Get onto the springboard of trusting Him every day of this year. You will bounce with joy unspeakable and will understand and experience for yourself what Isaiah says in Isaiah 58:11: "The Lord will guide you always; He will satisfy your needs in a sun-scorched land and will strengthen your frame. You will be like a well-watered garden, like a spring whose waters never fail."

Prayer

Lord Jesus, place my feet on a springboard, from where I can take off to achieve Your dream for my life, this year and in the years to come.

Suggested Scriptures for Further Meditation

Lamentations 3:22–24   Psalm 84:11   Romans 15:13

CHAPTER 2

MORE THAN GOLD, MORE THAN PURE GOLD

It is time for you to act, Lord; your law is being broken. Because I love your commands more than gold, more than pure gold.

—Psalm 119:126–127

Gold is one of the most precious ornamental metals in international trade. Its daily value on the world's commodities market is keenly monitored by investors. The price of gold in many ways determines the health and strength of the world's greatest stock markets, including those of London, New York, Tokyo, Hong Kong, Zurich, and Frankfurt. Because the price of gold is relatively high compared to other commodities on the stock market, many prefer investing in gold.

In the Olympic Games, athletes who win gold in the various events are called Olympic gold medalists and Olympic champions. As a metal, gold not only glitters, but also has the enviable property of being resistant to rust. The more it is passed through fire, the purer and finer it becomes. God Himself has a special affection for gold, as it represents royalty, purity, and endurance. In Exodus 25, God asked Israel to bring Him an offering for the tabernacle. The first item on the list of offerings was gold (Exodus 25:3). In the rest of that chapter, every key object or article for worship of and service to God was either made of gold or overlaid with gold. God has a passion for gold. To underscore the purity, endurance, and value of marriage, gold is the metal of choice for wedding rings.

However, there is something more valuable than gold. In Psalm 119:127, the psalmist declares that he loves God's commands (God's Word) more than gold, more than pure gold. To the psalmist, life is the most precious asset one can own. What really defines life and determines the right course of a fulfilled life is one's unwavering commitment to the unadulterated Word of God. In the gospel of John 1:1–4, John introduced Christ Jesus as the Word of God who was in the beginning with God and through whom all things (including humans) were made; without Him, nothing was made that has been made. Thus, for life to be meaningful, it has to be bathed in and fueled and nourished on a daily basis by the principles, instructions, and counsel of the Holy Scriptures. Psalm 19:7–11 extols the preciousness of God's Word and concludes, in verse 11, "By them is your servant warned; in keeping them there is great reward." The dividends (rewards) received through obedience to God's Word supersede returns on investment in gold stocks.

When Jesus was tempted in the wilderness by Satan, He turned to the Word of God as His point of reference. Since Satan cannot abide the truth, and since the Word of God is true at all times, we stand on the best and surest ground to overcome the wiles of the Devil when we stick to God's Word as our rule. We live on a planet created through the Word of God. In the beginning, God created and fashioned the heavens and the earth through the Word of His mouth. Whenever God said, "Let there be," something came into existence. If the world came by His Word, then we can best live in the world by His Word.

God's Word has life in it. Jesus says that the Words He speaks to us are spirit and life (John 6:63). The Words of God have a supernatural component. No one who has acted on the basis of God's Word has been found wanting. Yes, the world may oppose you for siding with God's Word, but the world cannot overcome you. See how miners leave no stone unturned when digging for gold? Some of the world's richest goldmines in Ghana and South Africa are more than two miles below the surface of the earth, yet mining companies invest in the latest technology to send miners and excavators down to dig for gold. How much do we invest in God's Word, which is much finer than pure gold?

For Joshua, who had the onerous task of taking the people of Israel beyond Jordan into the Promised Land, every military move was to be anchored by the Word of God. In Joshua 1:8, God told him, "Keep this Book of the Law always on your lips; meditate on it day and night, so that you may be careful to do everything written in it. Then you will be prosperous and successful." God had laid the foundation for success. As long as Joshua kept God's Word, God made Joshua's way successful. In like manner, as we move towards various "promised lands" in our lives and ultimately to a destination beyond this world, we should be careful to take a clue from Joshua and others of his calibre, men and women with a mission and on an assignment, people who fought the good fight of faith and ran the race to take hold of the crown of eternal life that God has appointed for the faithful. Moses was said to have esteemed the reproach of Christ as greater riches than the treasures of Egypt. *Esteem* means to place value on something. The Word of God works better than gold for those who esteem it. If you don't esteem it, then it will not work for you. There is something finer than pure gold. It is the Word of God.

Prayer

O Lord God, I desire Your Word above all else. May I study and understand Your Word, walk in obedience to Your Word, and share Your Word with my family, friends, and neighbours.

Suggested Scriptures for Further Meditation

Psalm 19:10   Psalm 119:72–127   Proverbs 8:10–11

CHAPTER 3

BEYOND REACH

For as high as the heavens are above the earth, so
great is his love for those who fear him; as far as
the east is from the west, so far has he removed our
transgressions from us.

—Psalm 103:11–12

There is a well-known expression that is usually applied (with a
negative connotation) to a person whose moral character, state
of health, or any other aspect of his or her life has deteriorated
to a level considered too abysmal for any chance of recovery,
restoration, or repair. I am referring to the expression "beyond
reach." This expression may also be applied to the socio-
economic situation of a country devastated by prolonged civil
war, chronic economic hardship, or anaemic political instability.
Such a country is sometimes referred to as a "failed state."
Until Jesus appeared on the scene, the condition of the
man possessed by a legion of demons (Luke 8:26–39) was
considered "beyond reach." The family of this man had given
up on him. For individuals and countries described as such,
it takes the grace of God and the power of the Holy Spirit to

"restore the years that the locusts have eaten" and to bring forth to life again any "Lazarus dead and buried for four days"! We would dare believe God to turn around any "beyond-reach" situation and to restore hope.

But there are issues in our lives that need to be put beyond reach. For these matters, our God Himself takes the initiative to do it. An example is in the twelfth verse of Psalm 103, which reads, "As far as the east is from the west, so far has He removed our transgressions from us." Any student of geography knows that trying to travel around the globe by going from the east to the west or vice versa is a journey whose destination is never reached. The spheroidal shape of our world makes it impossible to locate where east ends and where west begins. What the psalmist is saying is that through the redemptive work of our Lord and Saviour Jesus Christ on the cross, the sins we have confessed and repented of have been removed from us and put *beyond reach.* Hallelujah! This means that if we confess and forsake any sin committed, then God not only forgives us but also takes away that sin, together with its guilt, and puts it beyond our reach in a file that is closed and irretrievable. No matter how many times Satan reminds you of that sin, know that God has put it *beyond reach.* As far as the atoning provisions of the blood of Christ are concerned, the docket containing that act of sin is no longer accessible or admissible. The case has been dropped by the blood of Christ into an unknown place, *beyond reach.* There is therefore no condemnation for those who are in Christ Jesus. Has Satan been tormenting you with the memory of an old sin that you have confessed and forsaken? Tell the Devil, "It's *beyond reach,*" and move on in your relationship with the Lord. This beyond-reach concept, within the context of Psalm 103:12, cannot be overruled by Satan. Pay no attention to Satan or anyone else who wants to dig up your past. By Christ's shed blood, our sins have been put *beyond reach.*

Prayer

I thank You, God, for sending Your Son to die so as to save me from my sins. By faith in the shed blood of Jesus, I take authority over any guilt being pushed through my mind by Satan, knowing that Christ's blood has taken away my sins and that He has cleansed me from all unrighteousness.

Suggested Scriptures for Further Meditation

Zechariah 3:9   2 Samuel 12:13   Isaiah 38:17

CHAPTER 4

CHARGES OVERRULED!

Then he showed me Joshua the high priest standing
before the angel of the Lord, and Satan standing at
his right side to accuse him. The Lord said to Satan,
"The Lord rebuke you, Satan! The Lord, who has
chosen Jerusalem, rebuke you! Is not this man a
burning stick snatched from the fire?" Now Joshua
was dressed in filthy clothes as he stood before the
angel. The angel said to those who were standing
before him, "Take off his filthy clothes." Then he said
to Joshua, "See, I have taken away your sin, and I
will put rich garments on you."

—Zechariah 3:1–4

The Hollywood soap opera *L.A. Law* captivated the minds
of millions of viewers when it was first beamed on satellite
television networks across the globe a couple of decades
ago. Full of suspense, this show depicted some of the most
dramatic scenes in modern-day American courtrooms, where
the prosecution team and defense team battle over issues,
drawing out what each side believes is objective evidence for

why the judge or jury should find the accused person(s) guilty or not guilty of the charges.

What amazed me as I watched that series was the power of the trial judge, who, by virtue of his or her knowledge of the law and several years of experience, could agree or disagree with any point raised by either team. One could hear the trial judge shout, "Overruled," if he or she was not in agreement, or one could hear him or her say, "Sustained," if he or she agreed with a point raised by any of the teams. When all had been said and done by the defense and prosecution teams, the trial judge then pronounced judgment.

The Scripture verse quoted above is about a vision of a courtroom scene in heaven, captured and recorded in the Bible: God is the trial judge, the Lord (Jesus) is the defense lawyer, Satan is the chief prosecutor, and Joshua, a high priest, is the accused person. Satan, taking advantage of the sin of Israel at that time (represented by the filthy garments of the high priest Joshua), had rushed to the throne of God in heaven to file charges against Israel (the high priest Joshua). Satan had a rude shock when, after hastily levelling all his charges against Joshua, God rebuked Satan not once, but twice, and ordered that all the charges against Joshua be dropped.

In Revelation 12:10, the Bible refers to Satan as the "accuser of our brothers." Satan rejoices with passion when he sees a believer sin; with ungodly alacrity, he speeds off day and night to the throne room of God to bring charges against the believer. In another instance, Satan was before the throne of God to file charges against Job. Satan murmured against God, "Does Job fear God for nothing" (Job 1:8–9)?

Has the Devil filed some charges against you? When the prodigal son realized how wasteful he had been with both his inheritance and the dignity of his father's home, he repented and returned home. Little did he know, all along when he rebelled against his father and left home, that his father, dissatisfied with his rebellious behaviour, had made provision to receive him back as his son!

Our heavenly Father made a better sin-cleansing provision for us, through His Son Jesus Christ, even before the foundation of this earth. On Calvary's cross, where Christ shed His blood, God, merciful and gracious, put to rest, once and for all, the debate about sin, justice, and forgiveness. This is the way John put it: "My dear children, I write this to you that you will not sin. But if anybody does sin, we have one who speaks to the Father in our defense— Jesus Christ, the Righteous one. He is the atoning sacrifice for our sins" (2 John 2:1–2). Praise God, as there is ample provision for pardon and for cleansing our sins. Of course, this is not a licence to sin, but an opportunity to return, through repentance, to fellowship with the holy and righteous God, should our relationship with him go sour when, in our moments of weakness, we commit sin. We overcome Satan's accusations by the blood of the Lamb and by the word of our testimony. With the blood of Jesus, we prevail over Satan's charges and accusations.

Prayer

Thank You, Lord Jesus, for dropping all the charges brought against me by Satan. By Your atoning blood, I rejoice in the freedom You have given me.

Suggested Scriptures for Further Meditation

Hosea 14:1–2   1 John 2:1–2   Hebrews 8:12

CHAPTER 5

TALE OF LETTERS

> I also said to him, "If it pleases the king, may I have
> letters to the governors of Trans-Euphrates, so that
> they will provide me safe-conduct until I arrive in
> Judah? And may I have a letter to Asaph, keeper of
> the king's forest, so he will give me timber to make
> beams for the gates of the citadel by the temple and
> for the city wall and for the residence I will occupy?"
> —Nehemiah 2:7–8

Writing letters to friends, loved ones, kings and queens, bosses and subordinates, and sometimes even our enemies is a phenomenon as ancient and regular as sunrise and sunset. Many of us, I imagine, still remember the love letters we used to write and probably still write to our sweethearts, wives, and husbands. Millions of letters of application for jobs are written every day across the globe; letters of appointment to various positions are also written and dispatched every day. The information, communication, and technology age we live in now has even shortened drastically the time it takes for our letters, emails, tweets, WhatsApps, and what have you to reach relations. O the joy of receiving a letter of promotion to a higher position! It is something employees of all category long for.

In modern-day diplomatic circles, there is what is called a letter of credence, which governments issue to newly appointed ambassadors to be sent to the governments of their designated countries. In general, we all long for letters and mail of good tidings. Unfortunately, in the real world, we also receive in our mailboxes and email inboxes letters that convey bad news: letters of dismissal from jobs; letters conveying news of not being successful in an interview or on an examination; or a letter from a loved one opting out of an otherwise long-term relationship. Such letters or emails inflict emotional pain and can cause many tribulations and sleepless nights.

In biblical times, letters were also used to serve various purposes. It is very interesting how God took notice of all those letters. God still takes notice of all letters, emails, and texts sent and received by means of modern communication. So let all men and women, good and bad, great and small, know that God still takes notice of letters. God took notice of the letter King David wrote to Joab to mastermind the murder of Uriah (2 Samuel 11:14,15). God took notice of the letter Jezebel wrote to mastermind the murder of Naboth (1 Kings 21:8–11). Letters, for David and Jezebel, were tools that they used, by virtue of their high positions, to take by force what rightfully belonged to others. But God did not keep silent (2 Samuel 12:9–12; 2 Kings 21:17–19). When Sennacherib, king of Assyria, by virtue of his military power, wrote a letter to threaten Hezekiah, king of Judah, God took notice of that letter and acted decisively in defence of Hezekiah and Judah (Isaiah 37:14,15, 21, 36–38).

In order to fulfil His plans for the Israelites, God moved the heart of Cyrus, king of Persia, to issue a monarchial decree permitting the Jews to return to Israel after seventy years of exile in Babylon (Ezra 1:1). May God take away every reproach and restore you to where you really belong, your place of honour. Once these exiles settled in their new towns, they organized themselves to build a temple for the Lord, a cause worthy of praise. This, however, did not go down well with their enemies (Ezra 4:4,5). Sounds familiar, doesn't it? Try to improve upon your status in life and, sooner or later, Satan begins to organize a protest march against you! The enemies of the Jews resorted to an often-deployed satanic scheme by writing letters to the politicians of the day asking them to issue an order to stop the building of the temple (Ezra 4:11,17,23,24).

Your enemies may have succeeded, by means of letters and emails, in denying you of your promotion, job, inheritance, or intended husband- or wife-to-be. But cheer up, friend; God has the final say! He will surely show Himself strong on your behalf! The Jews in the book of Ezra did not give up. After a while, God turned the situation around in their favour. Another king (Darius) came to power and straightened the records. God will straighten all the records Satan has distorted to your disadvantage. King Darius, provoked by a letter written to him by the enemies of the Jews, issued a warrant to search the national archives, which resulted in the revelation that a royal decree promulgated years before had actually authorized the building of the temple for the Lord God (Ezra 6:1–5). Praise God! To show Satan, and the enemies of the Jews and your enemies, His awesome power, God moved King Darius to issue a decree ordering his enemies to stop interfering with the construction of the temple; the king went even further and directed that the cost of construction of the temple, including the wages of the workers on-site, be borne by the royal treasury (Ezra 6:6–12)! So the temple was built.

God shall similarly intervene in your case. All the letters and emails Satan has instigated to be written against you are hereby declared null and void by heaven's court of justice. Because of the royal decree written with the blood of Jesus, you should get ready to receive letters of credence, letters of promotion, letters and emails of appointment to positions of greater honour, letters and emails of invitations to important occasions, letters and emails authorizing kings and queens to grant your heart's desire, letters dismissing charges levelled against you, and letters compelling your enemies to shut up. This is a decree of divine order. Job 22:28 declares, "Thou shalt also decree a thing, and it shall be established unto thee: and the light shall shine upon thy ways" (KJV). Let the saints in Christ say, "Amen."

Prayer

By faith in Jesus' name, I overrule and set aside any written code or letter engineered in hell against my physical and spiritual well-being or against my career, my marriage, my finances, and my God-given dreams. May God compel to be written to me letters that favour His purposes for my life. In Jesus' name, I pray.

Suggested Scriptures for Further Meditation

Ezra 1:1–3   2 Corinthians 3:2   Daniel 6:10

CHAPTER 6

"AS THOU HAST BELIEVED"

Then Jesus said to the centurion, "Go! It will be
done just as you believed it would." And his servant
was healed at that very hour.

—Matthew 8:13 (KJV)

Many in our world today wish they had lived during the period
when Jesus walked physically in this world. For such people,
it would have afforded them a better opportunity to personally
call on Jesus to tell Him all their troubles, to heal them of all
their diseases, and to have Him touch them and set them
free from all of their infirmities. Such individuals, as we all
sometimes do, fall into the mood of saying, "How I wish Jesus
was physically present today to understand my concerns and
do something about them." May God have mercy on us!

By taking this attitude, we are saying in effect that unless
Christ is physically present, we cannot receive His healing
touch. Is He not the same yesterday, today, and forever
(Hebrews 13:8)? Is Christ not with us today? Yes, Christ is with
us today and will be with us forever. He lives, although He is
not physically present with us. The writer of Hebrews could not

have rendered it better as in Hebrews 7:25: "Therefore He *is able to save completely* those who come to God through Him, because **He always lives** to intercede for them" (emphasis mine). There were many who, in the days of Christ's physical presence on earth, saw Him and heard Him preach, teach, and heal the sick and those oppressed by evil spirits. Yet these individuals, because of their unbelief, did not receive the touch of Jesus' healing power. The book of Acts is a record of events that happened after Jesus ascended into heaven. In His name, the apostles healed people and set captives of Satan free. Jesus was not physically present. The apostles who preached the gospel believed in His name; the people who heard the apostles preach and teach believed in His name. The results were obvious: healings and deliverances from all kinds of troubles associated with humanity. Therefore, all of these wishes to have Jesus' physical presence as a panacea to our troubles have no basis. Also, they stem from secret unbelief we hide in our hearts. The Lord's promise is irrevocable: "Behold, I am with you always, even to the end of the age" (Matthew 28:20).

The Bible speaks about Jesus' not being able to do many miracles in His hometown, Nazareth, because, although He was physically present with the Nazarenes, they did not believe in Him. So the key to receiving Jesus' help to meet our needs lies in our unwavering expression of faith in Him by our words and actions. The Lord can do for us today what He did for those who lived around Him two thousand years ago, people who had the same challenges we face in our time. Such is the truth that cannot be twisted: Christ Jesus and, for that matter, God honours faith, regardless of who exercises faith in Him and when that faith is exercised. To the centurion who came to Jesus in Capernaum and who, in faith, said to Jesus, "Speak the word only, and my servant shall be healed," Jesus' response was, "Go thy way, and as **thou has believed,** so be it done unto thee" (Matthew 8:13; emphasis mine). And the result was that the centurion's sick servant who was not physically present with Jesus was healed the same hour the centurion believed that Jesus could heal him.

In Matthew 9:29, when the two blind men expressed faith in Jesus' ability to heal them, Jesus touched their eyes, saying, *"According to your faith* be it unto you." Was it Jesus' physical touch that healed the blind men? No. What, then, brought about the healing? It was the faith the blind men expressed in Jesus, which unlocked the healing power of Jesus to effect their healing. What did Jesus say to the blind men? *"As thou hast believed."* And their eyes were opened.

For what have you believed, or for what are you believing, God? You and I should by now know God's response to our expectations: *as thou hast believed.* Is that all? Yes, that is all! When the centurion believed with his heart and expressed with his mouth that Christ Jesus' word could heal his servant, the ball was no longer in the centurion's court, but rather in Jesus' court. Jesus did not fail. Instead, He honoured the centurion's expressed faith. If you have also believed with your heart that God can do something for you and you have confessed it with your mouth audibly, in prayers with thanksgiving, then the ball is no longer in your court. It is in the Lord's court. When we put money into our savings accounts, we do not need to go to the bank every day to verify whether the money is still safe. It is safe and collecting interest! Your faith in God is a worthy return on investment, for no one, Scripture says, has put his or her trust in God only to be put to shame. "As thou have believed" is the differentiator between all humans and God, for God cannot lie. As the Scripture says, "Let God be true and every man a liar" (Romans 3:4). This is what differentiated Mary from Zachariah and what differentiated the thief who was crucified with Jesus whom He saved from the one who was damned. It will differentiate you today. *As thou hast believed, so be it unto you.*

Prayer

I activate and stir up my faith in You, O Lord, knowing that You are the same yesterday, today, and forever. Help me, Lord, to live by faith and not by sight.

Suggested Scriptures for Further Meditation

Acts 9:34   Mark 9:23   Luke 8:48

CHAPTER 7

VIGIL IN HONOUR OF THE LORD

Now the length of time the Israelite people lived in Egypt was 430 years. At the end of the 430 years, to the very day, all the Lord's divisions left Egypt. Because the Lord kept vigil that night to bring them out of Egypt, on this night all the Israelites are to keep vigil to honour the Lord for the generations to come.

—Exodus 12:40–42

For many churches and Christian fellowships in many parts of the Christian world, the last Friday of every month is characterized by a night of prayer, beginning from about 9:00 p.m. and lasting until the dawn of the following Saturday. Popularly dubbed "all-night," many Christians observe this vigil (night watch) with passion and piety accompanied by powerful praises and prayers. We are forever grateful to God, because many of us who used to dance the Friday night away in nightclubs amidst drunkenness and dismal moral incorrectness have "seen the light" and would rather keep vigil in the temple of the Lord on Friday night than be someplace else where ungodliness reigns. Hallelujah!

Great revivals and good things have happened at these vigils. Great interventions—what I would like to call the "move of the Lord"—will continue to happen at these vigils. I vividly remember that it was during one of these night watches in March 1979 when I received "unction from on high"—a mighty outpouring of the Holy Spirit—upon my life. Since then, I have never looked back. I have been growing up in faith and strengthening myself in the service and worship of my Lord and Saviour Jesus Christ. Get yourself ready for the next vigil at your local church.

God continues, in many situations, to literally "move at night" to bring deliverance and help to His people. For the people of Israel, keeping vigil is not just a religious commitment, but also a commemoration to honour the Lord, "who kept vigil that night to bring them out of Egypt" (Exodus 12:42). In other words, there is a night that, for generations past and generations to come, the people of Israel have kept and will continue to keep: a vigil in honour of their God who delivered them from 430 years of bondage and humiliation in Egypt. Do you know how many vigils God has kept to ensure your being alive, to keep your business flourishing, to stay the Devil's hands off you, to frustrate the plans of your enemies, to divert a storm intended to sweep you off course, to turn the counsel of your secret foes into foolishness, to keep your footsteps away from traps hidden in obscure places, and to open doors of opportunity in your life? In Psalm 91:5, the Bible talks about the *terror by night*. I have learned over the years never to be frustrated if, when in bed at night, I find it difficult to sleep. For me, it might be a call to keep vigil for God so that He may intervene on my behalf or on the behalf of somebody else.

What a mighty God we serve—a God who keeps vigil to bring His people out of trouble! Of course, we know that the God of the heavens and Father of our Lord and Saviour Jesus Christ neither slumbers nor sleeps. But a night is coming, and may already be here, when God, figuratively speaking, will shed off sleep and stay awake throughout the night for your sake. For some people, a promotion at the office is long overdue, health is not at its best, finances are not in good shape, third parties have invaded their marriages, their children are under negative peer pressure, some of their neighbours hate them without cause, and so on. These are challenges that call for divine intervention, when all other efforts for amelioration of the circumstances have failed. One time in history, Daniel together with three faithful friends prayed all night long because Nebuchadnezzar had issued a death threat to Daniel and other officers in his kingdom. One time in history, Jesus prayed alone all night long till daybreak, because the Jews had threatened to kill Him. When danger looms, we all take necessary precautions, one of which is to seek God's face through prayer for guidance and protection. We sometimes do moonlighting—carry out a night job—to keep our finances healthy, don't we? It is therefore not out of place when a night is set aside for praise, worship, and prayer in order to secure victories over the tribulations of life. When God has given us the breakthrough, let us find something fitting to do in honour of the Lord. For some of us, we need to be at the next church night watch for the reason of getting out and honouring God with thanksgiving for the great things He has done for us. There is a great song by Helen Baylor with a lyric that goes like this: "If it had not been for the Lord on my side, tell me where would I be, where would I be?"

If the Lord had not set aside a night to keep vigil for you, then tell me where you would be now. After God's all-night session, the Israelites stepped out of Egypt to breathe the fresh air of freedom. In Exodus 13:4, God spoke to them and said, "Today, in the month of Abib, you are leaving." Somebody shout hallelujah! This is one of the most refreshing verses in the Bible. I can see somebody leaving behind, for good, years of reproach, humiliation, disappointment, tears of pain, and oppression of all kinds. This is your month of Abib; God has kept the vigil, and He says you are leaving Egypt for good! Egypt, in this context, represents anything that has held you back from reaching your God-inspired goal or kept you bound in a bad situation for a long time.

Prayer

I rejoice in and celebrate You, O Lord, for the countless vigils You have held for my sake, by which means You have not only delivered me from evil, but have also brought me to the path leading to my destiny. Teach me the art of keeping vigil in prayer until I win my battles, until a soul is saved and hope is restored to those in hopeless situations.

Suggested Scriptures for Further Meditation

Luke 6:12   Daniel 2:17–19   Acts 16:25–26

CHAPTER 8

BORN TO WIN

For everyone born of God overcomes the world.
This is the victory that has overcome the world,
even our faith. Who is it that overcomes the world?
Only he who believes that Jesus is the Son of God.

—1 John 5:4–5

I guess for many who tap their feet to the rhythm of reggae music, the track "Born to Win" still stirs up memories of the early 1970s, when Jimmy Cliff was the reigning monarch of reggae. I don't know your stake on the title of that track, whether or not you are born to win. Who is born to win? The truth of the matter is that whosoever is born of God is indeed born to win; he or she is born to overcome the world. What a powerful statement of faith! And how many of us are walking daily with that in mind, knowing that by believing that Jesus is the Son of God, we are on the winning side of this life on earth?

Jesus came all the way from heaven to earth on a mission to rescue humanity from its fallen state and to restore humankind to their God-purposed roles, positions, and entitlements. God was unequivocal when He said, "Let us make man in our image, after our likeness: and let them have dominion over the fish of the sea, and over the fowls of the air, and over the cattle, and over all the earth and over every creeping thing that creeps upon the earth" (Genesis 1:26). Backed by the blessing of God, we were positioned to be fruitful and multiply; to replenish the earth and subdue it; and to have dominion over the air and the sea, and over the earth. This was the status quo until we, then represented by Adam, let go of our rights and responsibilities, through our disobedience, which Satan capitalized upon to his advantage. Having lost ground to the Devil, the founder and general overseer of everything ungodly and evil, we became subject to him instead of exercising dominion over him.

But as a friend of mine used to say, "Absaloms don't last long in the palace," this in reference to Absalom, King David's son, who, through scheming and treachery, drove his father out of the palace in Jerusalem so that he could assume position as king, but for only a short period (2 Samuel 15–18). Yes, the Absaloms don't last long in the palace! Be encouraged; if there is any Absalom in your life, then know that his or her days are numbered. You will regain your position, which that "Absalom" has, by force or through scheming, taken away from you. And so it was that Jesus, the Son of God, came to break the yokes and the bonds by which Satan kept us under his control, against the agenda that God had purposed for us in the garden, the cradle of creation. God sent His Son. This Son of God, who is our Lord and Saviour Jesus Christ, was with His Father at the time of the creation of heaven and earth. He was part of the divine Trinity who said, "Let us make man in our image." Armed with the power to turn darkness into light, and wearing the full armour of the Godhead, Jesus mounted the cross. By His death, Jesus blotted out the handwriting of ordinances that were against us, that were contrary to us, and took them out of the way, nailing them to His cross. Having spoiled principalities and powers, He made show of them openly, triumphing over them (Colossians 2:13–15). By this way, the Devil, who invaded our privacy in the garden of Eden, was thrown out so that we, the original rightful managers of the garden, could be reinstated.

Therefore, if anyone be in Christ, then he or she is a new creation; he or she is reinstated and empowered to be fruitful and to multiply, to replenish the earth and to subdue it, and to have dominion over the things of the air, things in the sea, and things on the land. The Bible cannot lie: Whosoever believes that Jesus is the Christ is born of God, whosoever is born of God, overcomes the world. Are you born again? If so, then you are born to win the battles of this life. You are born through Christ to overcome the threats posed by Satan and sin. You are born to trample upon serpents and scorpions, the demonic creeping entities of this life, and all the powers thereof.

Do you know the power that is at your disposal as a child of God? Have you ever given deep thought to God's promise that He will give His angels charge over you? Tell me and show me where in the Bible is it written that some believer of God in the company of angels lost a battle or was overcome by unseen forces? Tell me. If men in earthly uniform can guard and secure royals and high-profile personalities (queens and kings, presidents and prime ministers, celebrities, and the like), then can you imagine what security surrounds us who are children of the Most High God and for whose sake angels are on assignment? The problem is that some of us are unable to appropriate these divine privileges into our thinking pattern and in our daily walk. The average Christian therefore sees himself or herself as being pursued and chased around by demons and witches, rather than the other way round: seeing himself or herself pursue, scatter, and chase demons away.

We are born to win. John, the Beloved Apostle of Jesus Christ, put it this way: "Ye are of God, little children, and have overcome them: because greater is He that is in you, than he that is in the world" (1 John 4:4). You are an overcomer by way of divine birth; you are an overcomer by way of divine right. When the army of Israel saw that Goliath had fallen by the stone of David, they arose to pursue the fleeing Philistine army. Our Christ has floored the Devil; let us arise and pursue, chase out, and strike down every satanic entity and power.

Romans 5:17 is a wonderful example of our victory in Christ. It acknowledges humanity's loss of heritage to Satan and reinforces the gain through Jesus with the phrase, "Much more they which receive abundance of grace and of the gift of righteousness shall reign in life by one, Jesus Christ." We are not born just to win but to reign as kings and priests unto our God. Stand up; stand up for Jesus, ye soldiers of the cross. It is time to lift up the royal banner. It must not suffer loss. From victory to victory, our Christ is leading us till every foe is vanquished. You are born to win.

Prayer

I thank You, O Lord God, for the victory wrought for me by the Lord Jesus in order to position me for productive, progressive, and purposeful living. I am born of God and therefore have overcome in the Lord. In Christ Jesus, I am born again; I am born to win and born to reign.

Suggested Scriptures for Further Meditation

1 Corinthians 15:57   John 16:33   Luke 10:18–19

CHAPTER 9

"SUCH AS I HAVE ..."

Then Peter said, "Silver or gold I do not have, but
what I have I give you. In the name of Jesus Christ
of Nazareth, walk."

—Acts 3:6

We live in a world of haves and have-nots. This is true. There
are things we have or possess, and there are things we neither
have nor possess. Permit me to ask you, what do you have?
Many of the troubles in our world today, I believe, stem from
the fact that the majority of us concentrate on and wish for
what we don't have rather than focusing on and maximizing the
potentials and benefits of what we already have. I challenge
you to change your focus from what you don't have to what
you already have. Peter told the cripple at the beautiful gate,
"Silver and gold have I none; but *such as I have,* give I thee."

We cannot give what we do not have; we can only give
what we already have. And God in His wisdom has placed
in all our hands that which connects us to our blessings and
can overflow into other people's lives as a blessing. By God's
standards, you are what you have; you are not what you don't

have. Your next miracle or promotion in life is linked to what God's providence has already placed in your hands. He has given you what it takes to reach your pinnacle of success. Many of the life-transforming, soul-touching stories in the Bible happened because God dealt with the personalities involved on the basis of what they had in their hands. In Exodus 3, we see Moses' encounter with God in the burning bush. This Moses was haunted by his past life and was chewing away the time as shepherd of his father-in-law's sheep. This was a man born and raised in the palace of the greatest king and kingdom on earth at that time. But disillusioned by difficult circumstances, Moses had become a hireling of somebody's sheep. It was a gruelling life in a wilderness, one which, many Bible commentators believe, played a key role in softening Moses' heart and preparing him to lead a people who were as stray-prone as his father-in-law's sheep. As God spoke from the burning bush to Moses about the assignment of leadership He had for him, Moses' body language and verbal responses to God's call gave hints of a person who felt he was not qualified for the job. Why? Moses focused on what he didn't have and what he couldn't do. So God, in Exodus 4:2, asked Moses, "What do you have in your hand?" Moses replied, "A staff." By that response, a whole new exciting and glorious chapter opened in Moses' life, through what God did with the staff that Moses had in his hands. With the staff, Moses brought Pharaoh to his knees; when Moses stretched that staff over the Red Sea, it divided the water so that the Israelites could walk through the sea on dry ground. When he held high the staff in his hands on a mountain in Rephidim, Joshua and the army of Israel defeated the Amalekites, who attacked Israel (Exodus

17). What do you have in your hands? This is the question awaiting your response.

During one of the severest famines recorded in Bible times, God sent the prophet Elijah into the life of a widow in a town called Zarephath in Sidon. During that time of food and water shortages, the prophet asked the widow for water and bread (1 Kings 17:7–17). The widow's response, paraphrased, was: "Look, I don't have any bread; *all that I have* are a few grams of flour and millimetres of cooking oil, just enough for today and no more." Elijah prophesied over *what the widow had,* and the result was the miracle of food for every day of the rest of the famine period. What do you have?

During these times of recession in many countries and financial depression in many homes, we are tempted to moan and cry about what we need, about what we don't have. So it was for a widow in the days of Elisha whose dead husband had left huge, crushing debt behind (2 Kings 4:1–7). When she cried out to Elisha the prophet for help, he replied to her, "How can I help you? Tell me, *what do you have* in your house?" I believe one of the reasons some of us are struggling financially is that we have neglected and ignored what we already have: our talents, opportunities, networks, positions we occupy in offices, qualifications and skills, friends and relations, etc. The prophet Elisha, under the anointing of the Holy Spirit, instructed the widow on what to do with what she had, a little flour and oil. By her obedience to the prophet's direction, her financial situation was turned around. She paid off all the debts and still had enough money to look after herself and her children.

One time in the days of Jesus, a crowd had been so glued to His soul-searching teaching that they lost consciousness of time, missing their lunch. As evening approached, they had eaten nothing. Jesus' disciples came to Him and requested that the people be sent away to the nearby villages to buy themselves food (Mark 6:30–44). Jesus' reaction was that the disciples should give them something to eat. The disciples' response was that it would be a huge drain on the ministry's budget to buy bread for five thousand men, not to mention the women and children. (We ourselves live amidst an economic situation where budgetary allocations for social services are not enough.) Then Jesus asked, "How many loaves *do you have*?" Isn't it amazing that our Father in heaven always focuses on what we have, on what He has already given to us? By praying over *what they had*—five loaves of bread and two fishes— Jesus, miraculously, fed the crowd all their fill, leaving leftovers of twelve basketfuls of broken pieces of bread and fish.

The miracle at the Beautiful Gate in Jerusalem as recorded in Acts 3 happened because Peter knew *what he had:* the authority and power to heal the cripple. Therefore, he said, "Silver and gold have I none; but *such as I have* give I thee. In the name of Jesus Christ of Nazareth, rise up and walk." Your next miracle is linked to what you already have. You already have what it takes to break into the class of the wealthy, successful, and great. If nothing at all, you have ideas, creative ideas, to solve some of the challenges facing humanity. Arise, for you have sat too long with innovative ideas.

Prayer

Thank You, O Lord God, for the gifts and talents with which You have graciously endowed me. I commit myself to serve

You, God, and humanity with these endowments in all humility and in love. Open Thou my eyes to see other unknown gifts hidden in me, and help me develop and polish these gifts in the service of Your kingdom, my family, and the world at large.

Suggested Scriptures for Further Meditation

1 Peter 4:10   Matthew 10:8   Romans 12:6–8

CHAPTER 10

PICTURES FROM HEAVEN

When the Son of Man comes in his glory, and all the angels with him, he will sit on his throne in heavenly glory. All the nations will be gathered before him, and he will separate the people one from another as a shepherd separates the sheep from the goats. He will put the sheep on his right and the goats on his left. Then the King will say to those on his right, "Come, you who are blessed by my Father; take your inheritance, the kingdom prepared for you since the creation of the world. For I was hungry and you gave me something to eat, I was thirsty and you gave me something to drink, I was a stranger and you invited me in, I needed clothes and you clothed me, I was sick and you looked after me, I was in prison and you came to visit me."

—Matthew 25:31–36

Very few people have ever been to the moon and walked on it. Over a period of three and half years, a total of twelve men landed on the moon. This was accomplished by two US pilot–astronauts' flying a lunar module on each of six NASA missions, starting on 21 July 1969, with Neil Armstrong and Buzz Aldrin on *Apollo 11,* and ending on 14 December 1972, with Gene Cernan and Jack Schmitt on *Apollo 17.* Neil Armstrong was first to set foot on the lunar surface, and Cernan was the last to step off it. In each of the *Apollo* lunar missions, there was a third crew member who remained onboard the command module.

When Neil Armstrong stepped on the surface of the moon, an estimated five hundred million people worldwide watched the event, the largest television audience for a live broadcast at that time. Equipped with sophisticated cameras, these lunar missions have sent back to earth thousands of pictures showing the surface of the moon with its picturesque features. The scientific information gathered from the moon together with the pictures have made it possible for the rest of us who have not been there to literally describe how the lunar surface, its climate, and atmosphere feel and look. It is almost like saying that we've all been there! Such is the power of science and technology. In recent times, we have even seen the surface of Mars, Jupiter, and Venus!

What about heaven, the heavenly abode of God the Father and His innumerable hosts of angels, the place whereof Jesus said there are many mansions prepared for occupation? Do we have pictures or scenes from heaven describing life there, events there, and who and what is there or who can go there? I have heard several stories about people who said they dreamt or fell into trance and saw heaven. I will not question some of these stories. The apostle Paul, for instance, speaks about knowing of a man who was caught up to the third heaven (2

Corinthians 12:2). In Acts 7:56, Stephen, upon being stoned (and dying soon thereafter), said that he saw heaven open and the Son of Man standing at the right hand of God. These and many other accounts in the Bible transmit to earth the best pictures from heaven, which orient us in the best position to "see" heaven and to describe life and events there. Some of these events are futuristic (depicting life in a future time) and serve as a caution to us on how to live whilst we are here on earth. So, like the moon, we may not have gone there yet, but the pictures we see from heaven today via the Bible should guide us in our preparation for heaven. The Bible is like a camera transmitting live pictures of events from heaven, where God dwells and operates from.

One of such events is the subject of the Bible quotation beginning this chapter. Jesus says a day is coming when He will sit on His throne in heavenly glory and people from all nations, from Angola to Zimbabwe, will gather before Him. He goes on to say that He will separate the people one from another as a shepherd separates the sheep from the goats. He will put the sheep on His right and the goats on His left. Then He will reward those on the right with eternal blissful life, whilst those on the left will be sent away to eternal punishment. If Jesus had stopped the camera from shooting more pictures at this point, then there would have been pandemonium and panic on earth, and turbulent theological debates as to who are the sheep and who are the goats.

So Jesus kept the camera rolling, providing more eventful pictures. As a result, more drama unfolded. Jesus, the King seated on His judgement throne, talks about how He had been treated by the two groups. The picture we are receiving from heaven is depicting a judgement day that is fast approaching, one when the righteous will be separated from the wicked. Interestingly, both sides of the divide or separation expressed surprise at the way Jesus said they treated Him; they treated Him differently. How are you treating Jesus today? On judgement day, the key questions will be these: What did you do to Jesus in response to His love, evidenced by His dying to pay the penalty for your sins? What did you do with His righteousness, which He imparted to you? How many lives did you touch with the love of the Lord?

Prayer

Lord, help me live today and every day with eternity in mind. Enable me to walk in accordance with Your will and to remain faithful to You till I appear before Your holy throne. Help me share Your love liberally with as many as I come in contact with, to bring comfort, help, and other support as the need may be.

Suggested Scriptures for Further Meditation

Revelation 20:11–12   Acts 7:55–56   Daniel 7:13–14

CHAPTER 11

CASTING OUT, CASTING DOWN, CASTING UPON

Casting all your care on him because he careth for you.

—1 Peter 5:7

For the weapons of our warfare are not carnal, but mighty through God to the pulling down of strongholds. Casting down imaginations, and every high thing that exalted itself against the knowledge of God, and bringing into captivity every thought to the obedience of Christ.

—2 Corinthians 10:4–5 (KJV)

As the days, weeks, months, and years roll by, one wonders what individuals do with these irretrievable periods of time before they slip into history. One wonders what we've been doing all this while. If nothing at all, I believe that during this time of the year, we are doing everything possible with God's help to fare better than we did in the same period last year. In an answer to the question "What have you been doing all this while?", this is what a young business executive said: "I have been *casting out* demons, *casting down* imaginations, and *casting upon* the Lord all of my anxieties." What an answer—and how I wish we could all share in this answer! His answer gives us plenty of food for thought and brings to mind the apostle Paul's expository teachings on spiritual warfare, from which no Christian is exempted.

Demons! Imaginations! Anxieties! Nothing can be far from the truth if we could but daily confront demons, *evil* and *negative* imaginations, and anxieties in the manner prescribed in Scripture. If we did this, then we would soar to fulfil every God-ordained purpose for our lives. If we would deploy against these three troublesome tyrants the weapons of our warfare, which are not carnal but mighty through God, and pull down strongholds, then we would, I tell you, prevail over many tribulations and cut down on the millions of painkillers and sleeping tablets that many of the seven billion inhabitants of earth swallow every day to ease their pain, calm their nerves, and induce sleep.

Demon-induced problems require a demon-casting approach if they are to be eradicated. So Jesus said that in His name we shall *cast* out demons. He knows that demons will not move an inch unless they are *cast* out, that is, commanded to relocate by people who exercise authority in Jesus' name. Not only has Jesus given us the power to *cast* out demons, but He has also given us, as one of the gifts of the Holy Spirit, the gift of discernment of spirits to aid us in discerning the activities of and exposing demons. Whenever Jesus discerned the activities of demons and confronted them, they fled. Whenever the apostles discerned their activities and confronted them, they fled. Whenever we choose to discern their activities and confront them in Jesus' name, they flee.

For some people, life has come to a standstill: nothing seems to move in their favour or for their good. The reason, in some cases, is not far-fetched: Satan has succeeded in infiltrating their mindset, or thought-life, with impressions and perceptions about them that are contrary to God's views and purposes. Satan is therefore holding these people captive through their unfounded imaginations (i.e., mentally enslaving them) so as to cut them off from the mainstream of successful and triumphant living. When Satan tries to sow a thought of failure, defeat, sickness, death, divorce, etc., into our minds, the apostle Paul, in 2 Corinthians 10:3–5, tells us what to do: immediately reject that thought and neutralize it with an appropriate Word from the Bible that is the opposite of what the Enemy has thrown at us. Thoughts, whether negative (from Satan) or positive (from God), are seeds which, if entertained in the mind, grow to produce fruits characteristic of themselves. When the Enemy attacks your mind with thoughts of defeat and failure, *cast* such thoughts down and replace them with God's promises for victory and success from relevant portions of the Bible. This is why studying and knowing God's Word is a must for all believers, so that we are always armed to neutralize every devilish, imaginary thought. Cast the satanic imaginations down; yes, you can, in Jesus' name.

What a welcome relief that our God desires that we *cast* all our care (anxiety) upon Him, for He cares for us. If there is one thing in today's competitive world that eats away at joy, peace of mind, health, and robustness, it is anxiety. In Luke 21:34, Jesus said that worrying weighs the heart down. Jesus, therefore, asks a question: Which of us by worrying can add a single hour to our lives (Luke 12:25)? In Philippians 4:6, Paul exhorts us not to be anxious about anything. Thus, anytime you are tempted to worry about something, you should, as Peter says, *cast* that anxiety upon the Lord. You need not carry that burden; by faith, pass it onto the Lord. Additionally, when we come to terms with the truth of Jesus' Words in Luke 12:25, "And which of you with taking thought can add to his stature one cubit?", we will not stumble or lose our peace.

Have you discerned a demon anywhere? Cast it out in Jesus' name. Are you tormented by an imagination that drives you crazy and leads you away from God's purpose for your life? Cast it down in Jesus' name. Are you being drained by constant anxiety about matters beyond your control? Cast it upon the Lord.

Prayer

In the name of Jesus, I overcome demons, imaginations, and anxieties. I cast out demons; I cast down every thought and imagination that is at variance with God's plan for my life. In Jesus' name, I cast all my cares upon the Lord.

Suggested Scriptures for Further Meditation

Mark 16:17   Psalm 55:22   Matthew 6:25

CHAPTER 12

CELEBRATING THE
LORD'S PASSOVER

Take a bunch of hyssop, dip it into the blood in the
basin and put some of the blood on the top and on
both sides of the doorframe. Not one of you shall
go out the door of his house until morning. When
the Lord goes through the land to strike down the
Egyptians, he will see the blood on the top and sides
of the doorframe and will pass over that doorway,
and he will not permit the destroyer to enter your
houses and strike you down.

—Exodus 12:22–23

It is one of the most remarkable events recorded in the Old
Testament of the Bible. It was an act of God that brought to an
end 430 years of enslavement of the people of Israel by the
Egyptians. The people of Israel gained freedom when, under
the instruction of God through Moses, they killed lambs and
applied the blood to the lintels and to the two side posts of the
doors of their houses. This was after all of Moses' persuading
Pharaoh to "let my people go" had failed. When persuasion

fails, force is applied. Let Satan and all his cohorts know that our God still applies force when persuasion fails.

What happened in Egypt was a shadow of the act of salvation God meant for all humankind and which found its fulfillment when Jesus, the Passover Lamb of God, shed His blood on Calvary's cross. By faith in Jesus' name, we are saved, because Christ's blood is still in the saving mode. Satan and the hordes of demons should know by now that they cannot resist the power of the blood of the Passover Lamb. They also know that if they show any resistance to God's plan for our lives, then we will resort to intervention by the blood of the Passover Lamb. And as long as we celebrate the Passover as instructed by God in Exodus 12:24, echoed by Jesus in Luke 22:13–30 and by the apostle Paul in 1 Corinthians 11:23–26, the power of the blood of the Passover Lamb guarantees our victory over any form of satanic opposition to our right of freedom and our rights to God's best for us in this life and beyond.

Let us continue to celebrate the Lord's Passover during the annual church programmes on Good Friday through to Resurrection Sunday. Let us celebrate the Lord's Passover during the Lord's Supper (Communion service) organized regularly in our churches. But above all, let's celebrate the Lord's Passover every day of our lives through submission to God's will and expression of our faith in Christ and in His blood. When the people of Israel applied the blood of lambs to the doorposts of their houses, they were expressing faith in the blood.

During the observation of the first Passover by the people of Israel in Egypt, God told them that the month they celebrated (or observed) the Passover was going to mark the "beginning of months." Celebrating the Passover, therefore, creates an opportunity for fresh beginnings, a step onto a path that leads you to your destiny as God has purposed. For Israel, it was a step onto the path that led them to Canaan, their promised destiny. The first Passover broke the yoke that held the people of Israel from stepping into their destiny. Christ, our Passover Lamb, has been crucified; the yoke of oppression over your life has been broken. Step into your God-ordained destiny.

Celebrating the Passover opens doors for victory over enemies. During the almost forty years of trekking in the wilderness, the Israelites did not observe the Passover. But when Joshua and his people passed through the Jordan and faced Jericho, a city with thick walls, Joshua remembered to celebrate the Passover. What was God's response? He sent the commander of the Lord's army to appear to Joshua to give him the strategy for defeating Jericho (Joshua 5:10–15)! You see, whenever the blood of the Passover Lamb is shed, God secures deliverance and victory for those who apply that blood. Jericho's walls crumbled under the power of the blood of the Passover Lamb. There is power—wonder-working power—in the blood of the Lamb.

Many, many years later, Hezekiah became king of Judah after the death of his father, Ahaz. Hezekiah brought major religious reforms to Judah. He opened the doors of the house of the Lord, which his father had closed, and repaired them. He revived true worship of God and the fear of Him in the lives of the people. But above all, Hezekiah restored the proper celebration of the Passover, which had been abandoned by Israel for a long time (2 Chronicles 30:1–5). Later on, Hezekiah felt sick and God sent the prophet Isaiah to tell him that he would die. When Hezekiah heard the words of the prophet, he turned to God in prayer and pleaded for his life (Isaiah 38:1–3). In his prayer, Hezekiah asked God to remember how he had walked before Him in faithfulness and in truth and for the good things he had done in God's sight, including the restoration of the celebration of the Passover! You know what? God spared his life and added fifteen more years to it!

In Acts 12, Herod, stretching forth his hands to afflict and torment the church, had James killed and proceeded to arrest Peter, whom he then kept in prison. Peter's arrest happened during the week of Passover. But the church prayed whilst celebrating the Passover. In response to their prayers, through the blood of the Passover Lamb, God sent an angel to break the hold of Herod on Peter's life and set him free. We should not hesitate to celebrate our Lord's Passover in season and out of season. It is not for fun that Jesus instructed we of the church to commemorate the Lord's Supper as often as we can, in remembrance of Him. When we celebrate the Lord's death as prescribed by Him, we enforce our victory over Satan, sin, and sickness.

Prayer

Thank You, Lord, for loving me to the point of shedding Your blood to wash me of my sins and to free me from the power of Satan. Today and every day of my life, I celebrate the victory I have through Your name over demons, sickness, poverty, and ignorance. Through You, I am more than a conqueror.

Suggested Scriptures for Further Meditation

1 Corinthians 5:7–8   1 Corinthians 11:23–25   1 Peter 1:18–19

CHAPTER 13

SINGING HYMNS TO GOD

Speaking to one another with psalms, hymns, and songs from the Spirit. Sing and make music from your heart to the Lord, always giving thanks to God the Father for everything, in the name of our Lord Jesus Christ.

—Ephesians 5:19–20

It's been a pretty long time since I left primary school. Going back to memory lane to reflect on what it meant to be in school in those days, I wonder whether the current generation of children in primary school are really enjoying school life. In my day, most schools were under the canopy of church administration, so Christian faith and moral discipline of the highest unadulterated order sandwiched academic pursuit. I still have nostalgia for the Monday–Friday pre-class school assembly in the morning. It was almost a full church service. Each day, we prayed the Lord's Prayer, recited Psalm 23, sang hymns, and heard short sermons by either the headteacher or a teacher on duty. Thereafter was the inspection of pupils' school uniforms for tidiness and also inspection of fingernails, of haircut, and of teeth. Every non-conformer received corporal punishment. We then sang a fast-paced hymn and marched into our respective classrooms. At the close of the day was an evening school assembly, also marked with prayer and hymns. The hymns were our anthem. Such was the atmosphere: spiritually positive, anti-demonic, almost crime-free, highly disciplined, and highly motivational and conducive for both teaching and learning. My tongue is still rife with those hymns I sang forty-some years ago.

Hymns are effective tools for praise and worship; I do solemnly believe that singing of appropriately worded hymns creates an atmosphere of empowerment, leading people to push through, persevere, and prevail over unyielding circumstances. This is why we must maintain the place of hymns in our church services and individual devotional practices. The Bible not only encourages the singing of hymns, but also gives instances whereby in people's singing of hymns, God showed Himself strong on the singers' behalf. Also, He made a way for them when there was no way.

Our Lord Jesus Christ is our best example. As the day of His death by crucifixion drew near, Jesus not only intensified His prayers unto the Father, but He also sang hymns to press on to the cross to clinch victory for us. After Jesus partook of the Supper with His disciples in the upper room, the Bible records, "When they had *sung a hymn,* they went out to the Mount of Olives" (Mark 14:26). After the Supper and the singing of hymn, the Lord Jesus was "fired up" to pray more in Gethsemane, defy betrayal by Judas, remain resolute in the face of Peter's denial of Him, absolve His disciples for deserting Him, stay on course despite a dubious kangaroo-court trial at the hands of the high priests, and survive horrendous torture at the hands of Roman soldiers until He mounted the cross on our behalf to declare, just before He died, "It is finished!" Praise the Lord!

The apostles Paul and Silas have a testimony to share about the divine power inherent in the singing of hymns. In a dark dungeon where they had been imprisoned after being stripped, beaten, and severely flogged by a court order, they opted to do the unusual, an act uncommon to prisoners. With their feet fastened in the stocks, they prayed and *sang hymns to God* at midnight, loud enough so that the other prisoners heard (Acts 16:22–34). Can you imagine that?! God's response to their singing was precise, quick, and lethal (against the powers of hell): a precision-guided earthquake of divine origin was unleashed against the foundation of the prison, flew open all the doors, and loosed every prisoner's chain! Praise God!

The resources God has placed within our reach are many and include the right application of singing of hymns and spiritual songs. Paul says in 1 Corinthians 14:26 that the singing of hymns strengthens believers; he exhorts us to speak to one another with psalms, hymns, and spiritual songs and to sing and make music in our hearts to the Lord (Ephesians 5:19). What are your favourite hymns? Sing unto the Lord a new hymn.

Prayer

O for a thousand tongues to sing my Redeemer's praise. To You alone, O Lord, I raise my voice to praise and honour You all the days of my life. I sing in joy to celebrate Your goodness towards me in this land of the living.

Suggested Scriptures for Further Meditation

Psalm 98:1   Colossians 3:16   Psalm 146:1–2

CHAPTER 14

STIRRING UP THE GIFT

Do not neglect your gift, which was given you
through prophecy when the body of elders laid their
hands on you.

—1 Timothy 4:14

For this reason I remind you to fan into flame the
gift of God, which is in you through the laying on of
my hands.

—2 Timothy 1:6

God created us as unique individuals. Even identical twins
are not alike in the true sense of the word. Each person's
genetic code is never duplicated by God to be shared with
another person. In this regard, there is no one like you! David,
with this understanding through revelation by the Holy Spirit,
wrote in Psalm 139:14, "I praise you because I am fearfully
and wonderfully made; your works are wonderful." You were
custom-made by God to serve a specific purpose or purposes
in this life; for this reason, God ensured that you did not come
into this life empty-handed. God has endowed you with natural

gifts and talents. Upon your new birth in Christ Jesus, God adds the gifts of the Holy Spirit so that you can find true fulfillment in your life on earth as you express your gifts and talents.

What has become of your gift(s)? Have you discovered or identified your gift(s)? And what are you doing with the gift(s), natural or spiritual? In chapter 9 of this book, we asked the question, what do you have? We all have something called *gift* or *talent.* The difference lies in for what purpose each of us deploys the gift whilst we live. In one of the parables that Jesus taught, a servant chose to bury his talent in the ground (Matthew 25:25). Where is your gift? Almost everything we use or enjoy in this life—the various means of transport, the myriad of electronic gadgets, the garments of all sorts, the houses we live in, the mouth-watering dishes we eat, the great goal scored by Asamoah Gyan of Ghana or Lionel Messi of Argentina, etc.—are all the outcomes of the deployment of the gifts and talents of those who have identified their gifts and have kept them alive against all odds and challenges, and through all the changing scenes of life, whether pleasant or unpleasant. The dress you are wearing, the wristwatch on your arm, and the mobile phone on which you just received a call are all expressions of gifts, human talents, or ideas that have been translated into tangible realities. Are you expressing your gifts?

The worst tragedy in life is to live without discovering your talent; neglected or underutilized talents are a form of human tragedy that have cost humanity. But a gift, when discovered, nurtured, and deployed into proper use, brings rewards first to the gifted individual and then to the rest of humanity. Cristiano Ronaldo is rich and famous because soccer fans are prepared to pay high gate fees just to watch him dribble the ball through the legs of the defenders of the opposing team and then slam the ball into the net. The story is the same for the gifted pharmacist, surgeon, musician, lecturer, drummer, cyclist, fashion designer, sculptor, Bible teacher, evangelist, actor, painter, et al.

The apostle Paul, spiritual father and mentor of a young pastor by the name of Timothy, did not want the latter to fall victim to the temptation and tragedy of wasted gifts. Therefore, in 1 Timothy 4:14, Paul admonished Timothy, "Neglect not the gift that is in thee." In this sense, Paul was making reference to the spiritual gift from God that qualified Timothy to serve in the office of pastor. The same principle applies to every living soul on earth: we should not neglect the gift God placed in us when He defined our uniqueness in our mother's womb. Neglect of one's gifting is an ingredient of a frustrated life. In 2 Chronicles 29:11, Hezekiah made a similar call to the priests and Levites not to neglect their assignments. A person's gift defines his or her assignment on earth. The apostle Paul went further in 2 Timothy 1:6, reminding Timothy to "stir up the gift of God which, is in thee." It was a father's call to a son to fan into flame God's gift in him, to rekindle it. This gift is represented here by the notion of a fire, which, if it be not frequently stirred up and fresh fuel added to it, will go out. A gift is like fire; it needs a constant supply of fuel to burn more brightly. Timothy, I believe, stirred up the gift by reading, meditation, and prayer, and by the frequent exercise or expression of his gift.

How are you stirring up your natural and spiritual gifts? How are you expressing your uniqueness through the gift God has placed within you? Stir up the gift.

Prayer

In prayer and through faith in Your holy name, Lord, I stir up the gifts You have deposited in me; I release myself from every hindrance to the manifestation of these gifts. I thank You, Lord, for hearing my prayer.

Suggested Scriptures for Further Meditation

Proverbs 18:16   Exodus 31:1–5   1 Samuel 16:18

CHAPTER 15

RANSOMED, HEALED, RESTORED, AND FORGIVEN

When you were dead in your sins and in the uncircumcision of your flesh, God made you alive with Christ. He forgave us all our sins, having canceled the charge of our legal indebtedness, which stood against us and condemned us; he has taken it away, nailing it to the cross.

—Colossians 2:13–14

There it stands: the cross of Calvary. For over two thousand years, it has endured every persecution, misrepresentation, mockery, ridicule, and intense hatred by Satan. Satan's goal is to deny or play down the relevance of the cross to shaping the history of humankind. Some kings, queens, emperors, and empires of bygone years, and their remnants in our time, have, inspired by Satan, tried but in vain to wipe out the memory of the old rugged cross from the affairs of humankind. Why would Satan vent so much venomous anger against the tree upon which Christ died? It is because by His death on the cross, Jesus broke the yoke of sin and death, by means of which

Satan had kept the whole of Adam's race under bondage (Hebrews 2:14–15).

This cross cannot be seen physically today, but its transformational impact on men and women, boys and girls, nations and generations past and present who have yielded and surrendered to the One who died on the cross, is phenomenal. The cross is the altar upon which God the Son, the Son of God, offered His life as a ransom for our salvation. It was on this cross that He proclaimed with the voice of triumph, "It is finished." This proclamation by Christ vibrated and echoed into all realms: the heavens, the earth, and the deepest portions of hell. It announced the redemption of humankind from the ruthless rule of Satan and from every form of affliction imaginable and attributable to Satan, who, through grand deception, took away from Adam our divine right to fellowship with God and our authority to reign in life on earth.

Easter and Passover should therefore be a time of joyous celebration. It is the joyous remembrance of the death that brought us life. That is why the day when Christ was crucified is befittingly called Good Friday. On that day, Jesus was pierced for our transgressions, crushed for our iniquities, and chastised that we might have peace. By His stripes, we are healed. Anyone who accepts His sacrifice on the cross is *ransomed, healed, restored, and forgiven.* We have redemption through His blood (Ephesians 1:7). By His precious blood, He purchased us (1 Peter 1:19; Revelation 5:9). The blood of His cross has power to cleanse and purge from our conscience dead works so that we may serve the living God (Hebrews 9:14). Jesus Christ is the real Passover Lamb. His blood, when applied by faith over any person or household, causes evil to divert its course away from those thereby protected.

The blood of Jesus that drenched the cross on Good Friday is vocal: it speaks. It is an interceding blood. Blessed are you if this sprinkled blood speaks on your behalf. The book of Hebrews says the blood that Jesus shed on the cross speaks of *better things* than the blood of Abel (Hebrews 12:24). It is about time you allowed the blood to cause a major shift in your life: *a shift from what is* good *to what is* best.

By shedding His blood on the cross, Jesus ushered in the new covenant to replace the old covenant (1 Corinthians 11:25). His blood causes an old, unproductive life to give way to a new, productive, and fulfilling life, for *if anyone is in Christ, then he is a new creation; the* old *has gone, and the* new *has come!*

How do you intend to celebrate Easter? Do you cherish the old rugged cross till your trophies, at last, you lay down? Will you cling to the old rugged cross and exchange it one day for a crown? Let's give Him praise and be forever grateful to Him, be forever grateful for the cross, be forever grateful that He came to seek and save the lost. Let's celebrate this and every Easter by singing this hymn:

> Praise, my soul, the King of heaven;
> To His feet thy tribute bring;
> Ransomed, healed, restored, forgiven,
> Evermore his praises sing:
> Alleluia, alleluia!
> Praise the everlasting King.

Prayer

I praise You, O God, King of the universe. To Thy feet my tributes I bring. You have ransomed me, forgiven me, healed me, and restored me. As long as I live, I will praise You. Into eternity, I will praise You. Hallelujah.

Suggested Scriptures for Further Meditation

Psalm 103:1–5   1 Peter 5:10   Jeremiah 30:17

CHAPTER 16

"I AM THE FIRST AND THE LAST"

When I saw him, I fell at his feet as though dead. Then
he placed his right hand on me and said: "Do not be
afraid. I am the First and the Last. I am the Living
One; I was dead, and now look, I am alive for ever
and ever! And I hold the keys of death and Hades."

—Revelation 1:17–18

When I was a young believer in Christ learning how to *walk
with the Lord,* I dreaded reading the book of Revelation, the last
book of the Bible. I used to be frightened by the descriptions
and events recorded there, such as the enormous red dragon
with seven heads, which had ten horns and wore seven crowns
(Revelation 12:3); a beast with ten horns and seven heads that
resembled a leopard but had feet like those of a bear and a
mouth like that of a lion (Revelation 13:2); seven angels with
seven last plagues (Revelation 15:1); and a woman drunk on
the blood of the saints, the blood of those who bore testimony
to Jesus (Revelation 17:6). But a lot has happened to my faith
between then and today. The book of Revelation is now one
of my most favourite books of the Bible.

The book of the Revelation of Jesus Christ is largely about events yet to take place both on earth and in heaven. What we did not know about Jesus from the gospels is revealed in Revelation. What Jesus did not say about Himself whilst He lived physically on earth, He has spoken in Revelation. One of such revelations about Jesus Christ is in Revelation 1:17–18: "I am the First and the Last. I am the Living One; I was dead, and behold I am alive for ever and ever! And I hold the keys of death and Hades." I believe that this is the basis for the Lord's unequivocal words of assurance that mark the beginning of verse 17: "Do not be afraid." He who conquered Satan, death, and sin at Calvary says we should not be afraid, even though we live in a world that is laden with uncertainties and fears. He speaks as One who is in full control over death and any circumstance in which you may find yourself. "Do not be afraid," He says to you.

What can we glean from His assertion that He is the first and the last? As the first, or number one, Jesus is before all things, and it is only in Him that all things hold together (Colossians 1:17). He is always the first to appear on the scene to aid us; we should therefore learn to occupy our minds with Him. He must be the first Person we think about or talk to when we awake every morning. Unfortunately for some people, their problems are the first things they think about when they awake; no wonder the rest of the day is controlled by those problems. But if we will learn to place Him first in our thoughts when we arise from bed, then He, Jesus Christ, the first and the last, the beginning and the end, will take charge from the beginning of the day and will see us through successfully to its end.

He must be the last Person you think about before retiring to bed. He is the last to leave the scene. When life's problems drag on for too long, human beings get fed up. A husband may get fed up; a wife may get fed up; parents may get fed up; families may get fed up—because the problem has brought them to their wits' end. A family's being fed up is why a man was abandoned by the pool of Bethesda for thirty-eight years. His family was around him for a few years, but when the situation got worse, they left him to his fate. But Jesus came to the scene as the last visitor the man ever had. Gracious me, Jesus lifted the burdens off the man's shoulders, returning him to normality (John 5:1–18). Jesus is always the last to leave the scene. He will not leave until He has resolved the problem.

Jesus holds the keys of death and Hades. A person who holds the key to a door controls access to that door. Such a person has authority over the room whose door key he holds. Jesus says that He has authority over death and over where people go when they die. You can entrust the totality of your life to Him. There are those who are so much afraid of death that sometimes, when they go to bed, they are unable to sleep for fear that they may die in their slumber. If that is you, then I charge you to shake off that fear, for Christ Jesus exercises authority and power over death for your sake. Death cannot intimidate you any longer. Jesus is the living One. Let's celebrate Him in worship.

Prayer

Awesome God, how great Thou art. Before the onset of time, You existed; when time ceases to be no more, Thou will continue to exist. Eternal God, help me remain connected to Thee so that I may enjoy the blissfulness of eternity with Thee.

Suggested Scriptures for Further Meditation

Hebrews 1:10   John 1:1–3   John 8:58

CHAPTER 17

GROWING UP IN THE LORD

And the boy Samuel continued to grow in stature
and in favor with the Lord and with people.

—1 Samuel 2:26

The desire of parents is to see their children *grow up* from the time of birth, through the childhood years and adolescence, and through the period as young adults who have completed college or university and are now working to earn income, build relationships that may lead to marriage, make a positive impact on society through purposeful living, become parents themselves who also want to see their children grow up, and leave behind generations who will keep the tradition. The cycle goes on and on and on until Jesus returns.

Our God, our Father in heaven, also desires to see us *grow up* and serve His purposes for our generation, passing the baton on to others who would intend to *grow up* and serve God's purpose for their generations. Within the context of this chapter, *growing up* means "developing into a stature, characterized by maturity and responsible behaviour, and having the capacity to function and serve in line with God's purpose for one's life."

In the book of 1 Samuel, a man by the name of Elkanah and his wife, Hannah, gave birth to a son called Samuel, whose life's trajectory as recorded in the Bible epitomizes *growing up:* growing up in the Lord to serve His purpose and to become an instrument of blessing to the whole nation and the world. Samuel's life was an expression of a mother's gratitude to God, a fulfillment of a vow a mother made to God when she was praying for a child, a male child (1 Samuel 1:11). So after Samuel was born and had been weaned, Hannah took the little boy to the house of God, to the priest Eli, and said, "So now I give him to the Lord. For his whole life he will be given over to the Lord" (1 Samuel 1:28). A seed remains a seed with all the potential embedded or locked up within it unless it is sown into good soil to begin the process of germination and then grow into a mature fruit-bearing tree (John 12:24). When Hannah "sowed" her son into the hands of the Lord, Samuel began a journey of growth into maturity and purposeful living that brought back on track the nation of Israel, which had, at the time, lost its bearing in the Lord. *Growing up* in the Lord begins with surrender, and it progresses with the daily surrendering of our lives completely to Him.

From the day his mother surrendered him to the Lord at the temple, Samuel, the Bible says, "worshipped the Lord there" (1 Samuel 1:28b). A growing Christian worships God in spirit and in truth. At a time when the priesthood in Israel had gone wayward, Samuel—a boy wearing a linen ephod (1 Samuel 2:18)—was described as ministering before the Lord. A growing Christian finds his or her place in the house of God to serve. What are you doing in your local church? With continuous physical, moral, and spiritual support from his godly parents, Samuel *grew up in the presence of the Lord* (1 Samuel 2:19–21). Parents, are we supporting our children? Children, are we *growing up* (enjoying, staying) in the presence of the Lord? When the moral fibre of Hophni and Phenihas, the priests at the time, was decaying rapidly, Samuel kept moral uprightness and *continued to grow in stature and in favour with the Lord and with people* (1 Samuel 2:26). A growing Christian does not follow the crowd or popular opinion, unless the crowd or popular opinion is right in the sight of the Lord.

Samuel *grew up* in the Lord because he respected the spiritual authority that God had placed over him for guidance and counsel (1 Samuel 3:1). Are you serving under the authority of a spiritual head, and are you submissive to your head? It was through the guidance of Eli that Samuel was able to discern the voice of God and respond to God's call (1 Samuel 3:10). Samuel *grew up* to the level of hearing God speak and reveal to him things that were happening and were about to happen. Can you hear God speak to you? Like a mature fruit-bearing tree, Samuel's spiritual growth and maturity became evident for all to see: God was with him as he *grew up;* God backed Samuel's words; all Israel recognized him as a prophet of God; God continued to reveal Himself to Samuel; and Samuel's word came to all Israel (1 Samuel 3:19–21; 4:1). The testimony about Jesus' birth and growth hit similar milestones. In Luke 2:52, the Scriptures say, "And Jesus grew in wisdom and stature and in favor with God and man." Keep *growing up!*

Prayer

As You grew up in stature and in favour with God and humankind, I cry to You, O Lord Jesus, that I may experience spiritual and physical growth that leads to maturity in God and that I may also fulfil the calling of God on my life.

Suggested Scriptures for Further Meditation

Luke 1:80   2 Peter 3:18   Hebrews 6:1–3

LEAPFROG

Let us then approach God's throne of grace with
confidence, so that we may receive mercy and find
grace to help us in our time of need.

—Hebrews 4:16

Amazing grace, how sweet the sound! I am reminded of the
famous hymn. Grace is divine; grace is godly; grace is of God.
I don't think we have the words to explain what it means. Grace
transcends human understanding. It is an attribute of God;
the Trinity alone exercises and expresses grace to its fullest
dimension. It is only the grace of God that brings salvation
(Titus 2:11), and that grace reaches us through the one and
only Jesus Christ (John 1:17). Grace justifies (Romans 3:24)
us, and grace empowers us to endure life's tribulations (2
Corinthians 12:9). It is the grace of God that lubricates life.
When you are under grace, your life cannot be veered off track
by any power of darkness.

Grace has made and continues to make history, for
whenever or wherever the grace of God abounds, uncommon
things happen: supernatural change takes place in situations

confronting people's lives. Grace has a track record of causing individuals to leapfrog. A frog does not walk; it leaps. To leapfrog means to vault over a hurdle; it means to make progress by large jumps, instead of in small increments. Leapfrogging leads to a change of location, from a lower place to a higher place. When the grace of God abounded towards the cripple at the gate called Beautiful (Acts 3), the Bible says the man jumped to his feet! All his life, this man had been crawling. Anyone who crawls can never compete with those who walk. Are you crawling in life? Behold grace! The grace of our Lord Jesus Christ caused the crawling cripple to jump to his feet and begin to walk. What a change grace brings!

When grace finds you, it transforms you: it changes your language; it changes your tastes; it changes your wardrobe; it changes your song; it changes your address; it leapfrogs you! The apostle Paul was a beneficiary of the power of grace. Hear him extol the manifold grace of God upon his life in 1 Corinthians 15:9–10: "For I am the least of the Apostles and do not even deserve to be called an apostle. ... But by *the grace of God* I am what I am, and *His grace* to me was not without effect. ... No, I worked harder than all of them—yet not I, but the *grace of God* that was with me." God's grace qualifies those disqualified by humankind.

I can see the right hand of David the shepherd-boy raised up as if to say, "I also have a testimony." The youngest of his father's sons, and not considered fit by his father, Jesse, to be in Saul's army, let alone be king over Israel, David had been sent away from home on the day the prophet Samuel went to Jesse's house to look for a prospective king among Jesse's sons. Even though David's own father dislocated him from the scene of coronation, the grace of God located him and brought him to the scene of coronation. The one considered unfit turned out to be the one chosen by grace to be king of Israel. By grace, David leapfrogged over his senior brothers to rule over Israel.

Another biblical character who was the recipient of God's grace was Ruth. Ruth had arrived from the land of Moab with her mother-in-law, Naomi, to Bethlehem in Israel. In Israel at that time, Jewish prejudice against the Moabites, who had been traditional enemies of Israel, was rife. With her faith solidly invested in God, Ruth, as recorded in the book of Ruth, began life in Israel as a collector of leftovers of grain at Boaz's farm. That identified her as poor, as the least qualified labourer on the farm, which already had "highly" qualified Jewish women at the forefront of the farming business. However, the underdog, Ruth, caught the attention of the farm owner, Boaz. When the grace of God comes upon anyone, it imparts distinction, making it impossible for that individual to be avoided or ignored. Boaz, therefore, could not avoid or ignore Ruth. He ordered her transfer from way back to the front line, where all the "highly qualified" women were harvesting the grains. As if that wasn't enough, Boaz soon fell in love with Ruth and married her. What happened? Grace enabled Ruth to soar over the other "more qualified" women to win the love of wealthy Boaz. No sooner than later, she was being addressed as "Madame" by all the workers on the farm. Grace exalts; grace repositions one into a better status.

When the grace of God found Mephibosheth, the son of Jonathan, living in poverty-stricken Lo Debar and barely making ends meet, King David ordered Mephibosheth's immediate transfer to the king's palace in Jerusalem, with the full rights and entitlements of a prince (2 Samuel 9). Grace can make the poor rich. May God's grace locate you and then relocate you to higher ground. A friend recently told me that grace is God's answer to an unfair world. God knows how unfair many events and happenings in life will be, so He has prepared His grace to counter that and to pour on us favours we don't deserve. May you find *grace to help* in your time of need, *grace to leapfrog. And may the grace of our Lord Jesus Christ, the love of God, and the fellowship of the Holy Spirit be with you.*

Prayer

O Lord God, promotion does not come from the east, nor the west, nor the south, nor the north, but from You. You are the God that raises up the poor from the dunghill and sets them among princes. Remember me, and by Your grace grant me an elevation unto a higher ground of honour and dignity.

Suggested Scriptures for Further Meditation

Galatians 2:9   Psalm 30:5   Jeremiah 1:5

CHAPTER 19

DISTINCTION BY DIVINE ORDER

I will make a distinction between my people and
your people. This sign will occur tomorrow.

—Exodus 8:23

I wonder how difficult or impossible it would have been for
us as humans to fathom who God was, who God is, and who
God is to be if there were no Scriptures in which God, through
His Spirit, had graciously chosen to reveal Himself to us. I
am bewildered by His ways and acts, especially His dealings
with us humans, who are the pivot of His creation. I am dazed
by His insatiable desire throughout all generations to show
Himself strong on behalf of those whose hearts are loyal to
Him. I am astounded by God's wisdom. To borrow from the
apostle Paul: "Oh, the depth of the riches of the wisdom and
knowledge of God! How unsearchable His judgments, and His
paths beyond tracing out" (Romans 11:33)!

If God chooses an individual and sets him or her apart
for His divine purposes, and when God chooses to lavish His
favour upon such an individual, the life of that person becomes

what can best be described as one marked with *distinction by divine order.* Wherever God chooses to locate and settle that person, the mark of distinction abides with him or her. Whatever path God decides to lead the person on, the mark of distinction accompanies that individual. Like Abraham's son Isaac, that person is able to bear plenteous fruit under any challenging circumstance.

The mark of distinction is the difference the Sovereign God makes between His chosen ones and all others. You may be wondering, *Who are these "fortunate" ones God has chosen?* For you who have given your life to Christ and therefore been made right with God by the blood of Jesus are, by divine ordination, chosen and set apart by God; the distinction by divine order is placed upon you (1 Peter 2:9; Ephesians 2:19; Psalm 4:3). Once you have placed your life into God's hands, His mark of distinction overshadows you and the tone is set for Him to make a difference in and with your life. Both history and contemporary times confirm that when God takes hold of a person, He makes a difference with that person's life, to His glory. Dear one, are you already in God's hands? If so, then do not fret nor fidget: stay put, and allow Him to make that difference in you.

In Bible times, as recorded in the book of Exodus, the people of Israel found themselves behind oppressive Egyptian bars for 430 years. When, as per God's plan, their moment of deliverance arrived, the powers that be in Egypt refused to lift the yoke of bondage off the shoulders of Israel, a nation sealed with God's mark of distinction. By acts unparalleled in the history of Egypt, God declared a war of judgement on the powers of Egypt, sending unimaginable precision-guided plagues. These were plagues that received instructions from on high to go on rampage in the whole of Egypt except the district of Goshen, where the people of Israel lived. God chose to deal differently with the district of Goshen where His people lived (Exodus 8:22–23). He told Pharaoh, "I will make a *distinction* between *my people* and *your people"* (emphases mine). Did you hear that, child of God? There is a mark of distinction that is designed through the blood of Jesus to differentiate you from those who are without Christ. When the plague on the firstborn struck, God, by means of the blood of the Passover Lamb, made a distinction between firstborn Israelites and firstborn Egyptians, even between firstborn Israeli cattle and firstborn Egyptian cattle (Exodus 11:4–7). God has not changed His stand: He knows those who are His; He still differentiates His own from others.

How dare, then, that ungodly people of today want Christians to be like them! No! And why on earth would any Christian born of the Spirit wish to be like the people without the Spirit? How can we, upon whom the glory of the Lord is raised, fail to shine? Shine, dear one. Shine and make a difference with the glorious light Christ Jesus sheds daily upon you. Our distinction or peculiarity as believers in Christ originates with God. Anyone who reveres the Lord, that is, fears the Lord, receives God's mark of distinction for special use as a vessel of honour. In Malachi 3:16–21, the truth about God's mark of distinction is stated clearly:

> Then those who feared the Lord spoke to one another, and the Lord gave attention and heard *it*, and a book of remembrance was written before Him

for those who fear the Lord and who esteem His name. "They will be Mine," says the Lord of hosts, "on the day that I prepare *My* own possession, and I will spare them as a man spares his own son who serves him." So you will again distinguish between the righteous and the wicked, between one who serves God and one who does not serve Him.

To distinguish means to make a distinction. As believers, God sets us apart; we are distinct. That is why Christ Jesus said that his disciples, in other words, believers in Christ, are the salt of the earth. Salt is distinct in that it imparts flavour to food. We can't afford to lose our taste. Our distinction is of divine order.

Prayer

You are crowned with distinction, O Lord. You are excellent in all your ways. Because of Your favour over my life, I will arise and shine, bringing glory to Your name. Mark me with Your seal of distinction that all may see it and give glory to Your holy name.

Suggested Scriptures for Further Meditation

Psalm 4:3   2 Timothy 2:20–21   Exodus 1:19

CHAPTER 20

ANGELS DESCENDING

The angel answered, "The Holy Spirit will come on
you, and the power of the Most High will overshadow
you. So the holy one to be born will be called the
Son of God."

—Luke 1:35

It is not uncommon to hear Christmas carols being played
in and around Christmas season. Some of these carols, or
Christmas songs, tell the story of the birth of Christ. They
are indeed great songs, many of them composed hundreds
of years ago. Even though they have been sung for several
centuries, they have retained their original spiritual freshness,
flavour, and sacredness. Lest we forget, the first Christmas
carol was composed by angels who, praising God for the birth
of Christ Jesus, said, "Glory be to God in the Highest, and on
earth peace to men on whom His favour rests" (Luke 2:14).

If there was one event recorded in the history of humankind
that involved the unprecedented participation of angels, it
was the birth of Christ. There was angelic involvement in the
periods before, during, and after His birth. One would not be

far from the truth in calling that period *the season of angels.* During that season, about two thousand years ago, flights between heaven and earth were fully booked by angels. What a privilege it was for us to have had angels descend upon this terrestrial ball we call planet Earth.

Angels, I believe, are still descending every day to carry out specific assignments. Do not be surprised if, one of these days, angels appear to you, as they appeared to people in biblical days, *with good news of great joy.* Amen! Yes, the angels descended with good news. May they come again and again with good news, to refresh this global village in which we live that is wearied by bad news. We pray to God to do it again, to send His angels to tell us *something* that will put a smile on our faces.

For Zechariah and Elizabeth, it was an angelic visitation that assured them that, although they were both aged, it was not too late for them to have a son, John. Are you afraid that time is running out for you for an expected breakthrough that seems endlessly far away? Hold on, keep hope alive, and God will surprise you: an angel of God is coming your way!

As for Mary, the virgin, the angel Gabriel pronounced a high-class favour upon her to the extent that she conceived and gave birth to the Messiah. Her status was changed by a single encounter with the angel. Such an encounter is still possible today. You will have an encounter of that dimension for your elevation and elation. You, too, will have a song, just as Mary had. In the event that you are saddled with a mind-boggling problem that is draining your peace, may an angel of the Lord appear to you in a dream, as he appeared to Joseph (Mary's fiancé), and show you the right step to take in the will of God.

Angels carry the glory of God. When the company of angels appeared to the shepherds watching their flocks by night, the Bible says that *the glory of the Lord shone around them.* May that be your portion: may God's glory shine on you to give you a competitive advantage in your career, business, education, and ministry!

In our world today, there are still "Herods" who cannot stand to see people blessed, and so they scheme and plan to carry out *genocide* with the sole aim of eliminating anyone they suspect to be too much blessed by God. Any Herod tracking your life will fail. Just like Joseph, the husband of Mary, God will cause an angel to appear to you in a dream to show you how to escape before your enemy strikes. Amen.

As you keep your focus on Jesus Christ every day, be assured that the angels who descended during the first Christmas are descending again to do you good. So celebrate every day in style as though it is Christmas, knowing that "angels from the realms of glory" are still on divine assignment, descending and ascending to minister to us, the saints in Christ Jesus.

Prayer

Let my walk, O Lord, in this life be associated with the company of thousands and thousands of Your angels in joyful assembly; let Your angels mount garrison around me, and let them do warfare against those who hate me without cause.

Suggested Scriptures for Further Meditation

Exodus 23:20   Luke 22:43   Hebrews 1:13–14

Chapter 21

Partners with God

For it is God who works in you to will and to act in order to fulfill his good purpose.

—Philippians 2:13

Since the dawn of creation, when God graciously made us in His image, creating us as male and female, God has always treated us as strategic partners in the execution of His divine plan for life on earth. A big God with great dreams seeks partnership with humankind to accomplish great things. What a privilege, then, for you to know that God's mantle of responsibility rests upon you to carry on multiple assignments whilst alive before being called home by Him for eternal rest.

So many people have come, played their part, and gone into eternity, awaiting God's great speech- and prize-giving day, which is scheduled to coincide with Jesus' second coming. What a day it will be this time, Jesus, not being born as a babe in a manger, but coming as the King of glory to judge both the living and the dead! In the same way that His first coming (birth) was prophesied and was fulfilled, so has His second coming been prophesied. It will surely come to pass (Acts 1:11; Revelation 22:7).

Noah did his part by building the ark; Moses led the people to the verge of Jordan; Joshua led the people across the Jordan into the Promised Land; Esther used her position as queen to rescue her people from death; the apostle Paul carried the gospel to the Gentiles of His time; and scores of missionaries defied death and danger to ferry the gospel across the oceans to Africa and the extreme fringes of the earth. Alexander Graham Bell invented the telephone to make it possible for us to talk over long distances; the Wright brothers made it possible for people to travel by air; Dr. Alexander Fleming, the Scottish scientist and Nobel laureate, discovered the antibiotic penicillin in 1928, placing into humanity's hands a biochemical weapon to fight pathogenic bacteria. In all these, God was in alliance.

These and many, many other great achievements are high-profile tasks. But the world has not come thus far by way of only high-profile achievers and achievements. Many other people, male and female, working behind the scenes, carrying out what in our finite thinking may be called low-profile responsibilities, tasks, and achievements, have equally been recognized and used by God to get the world thus far. Whenever God strikes alliance with a person, male or female, the end result is always a blessing to all humankind. So it was in the first Christmas story: God struck an alliance with a young couple relatively unknown by people, but seen, known, and chosen by God, to take up the mantle of great responsibility of being the earthly parents of Jesus Christ, the Son of God. What a great responsibility: to nourish, train, discipline, protect, guide, and guard Jesus from His time in the womb until He reached the age of thirty, in order for Him to carry out His divine assignment of laying down His life for the salvation of humanity! God did not commit the parenting of Jesus to angels but to a young, inexperienced couple (a first-time mum and dad). How did Joseph and Mary manage it all? How are we, in this twenty-first century, parenting the children God has given us?

We are in alliance with a God who is keen to see us succeed and accomplish any task He gives us. Knowing our fragility as humans, God comes around us with benevolence to enable us to cope with and triumph over the enormous challenges that accompany parenting and the many other demanding tasks that characterize life on earth. Indeed, He is our strategic Helper. When the controversy about Mary's pregnancy threatened her relationship with Joseph, God stepped in to counsel Joseph to stay in the relationship; when Mary went into labour in a fully booked inn in Bethlehem, God stepped in with provision of a manger; when King Herod threatened the life of baby Jesus, God stepped in and provided a way of escape into Egypt. Whenever our big God places a great responsibility on us, He stays by to see us through. He did not fail Joseph and Mary; He will not fail you. In all your responsibilities, remember who is near to help: God.

Prayer

Let my eyes always behold Your assignment for me here on earth, Lord. Let my hands remain on the plough until each task is accomplished. Let my feet be quick to go where You send me, and let me not return until I have paid my dues of service to You and for the good of humanity.

Suggested Scriptures for Further Meditation

Acts 13:2   Acts 26:16–18   Romans 12:6–8

CHAPTER 22

ROUGH START, GLORIOUS END

> Joseph also went up from Galilee, from the city
> of Nazareth, to Judea, to the city of David which
> is called Bethlehem ... in order to register along
> with Mary. ... While they were there, the days were
> completed for her to give birth. And she gave birth
> to her firstborn son; and she wrapped Him in cloths,
> and laid Him in a manger, because there was no
> room for them in the inn.
>
> —Luke 2:4–7

The long wait had come to an end: the fulfillment of what God promised in the garden of Eden about the seed of a woman coming to earth to live among people, bruise the head of Satan (the Serpent), and restore humankind to everlasting fellowship with God. I don't think Satan had full insight into the plan God had struck to bring about the birth of Christ through the Virgin Mary. If Satan had known the details, then he would have done everything in his power to abort the birth of Christ. Praise God, Satan did not know—and so it is and shall forever be that the

Devil will never know all the details of God's purpose for your life either! Your dreams will never be aborted!

The entry of Jesus to the world, though, was not without challenges and dangers. His beginnings were rough. Jesus was not exempted from the "baptism of fire" that appears to overshadow the start of many endeavours, programmes, businesses, marriages, etc. Do you remember the chaotic scenes that followed the grand opening of terminal 5 of Heathrow Airport in London a few years ago? Due to a failure in the operation of the computer systems that controlled sorting of luggage, many passengers spent hours on end trying to locate their suitcases and travel bags at the arrival terminal.

Jesus also shared in the frustrations of new beginnings, even right from the womb. First and foremost was his initial "rejection" by his earthly father-to-be, Joseph. But God made a way for Him to be accepted by Joseph. Then there was a royal decree from a governor requiring that Joseph and Mary (the latter then at full term with her pregnancy) travel a long distance, all the way from Nazareth uphill to Bethlehem, which is above fifteen hundred feet higher in altitude. Remember that there were no taxis, buses, trains, or aircrafts in those days. Yes, there were donkeys and camels, but consider a pregnant woman, at full term, riding on a donkey's back uphill, all the way to Bethlehem. But God gave Mary the strength to endure and to avoid delivery on the way. With no hospital and no midwives, Joseph, inspired by God, had to help Mary push and deliver the Messiah in the backyard of an inn where sheep and probably stubborn he-goats were kept! You and I know that where sheep and goats flock together, the laws of sanitation do not apply. The obnoxious, overpowering odour they generate cannot be subdued by any highly prized perfume in an alabaster box. But that was the environment wherein Jesus breathed in his first air after birth; that was where He began His mission on earth to pave the way for us to enter clean, fragrant, and sinless heaven, where the streets are made of gold. When was the last time you really thanked Jesus for the price He chose to pay to make you whole, to have your name written in the Book of Life, and to give you inheritance among all those who are sanctified?

How many more ordeals should a newborn babe endure? Soon, the news about Jesus' birth incensed Herod and the whole of Jerusalem. Herod, displaying the same traits as a modern-day, power-drunk undemocratic dictator, gave an order for all boys below the age of two years to be killed. But God, wiser and smarter than Satan and Herod and all our enemies, moved in quickly and instructed Joseph to take Mary and the baby Jesus to safety in Egypt, where Herod's rule of madness had no jurisdiction. Through it all, God showed His power to see the infant Jesus through all the fiery trials of His early years, His challenging beginnings. For the young couple, Joseph and Mary, God's faithfulness enabled them to cruise through all the storms of the early years of marriage and parenting to the day when their Son and the Saviour of the world, Jesus Christ, was glorified on the morning of His resurrection.

Somebody somewhere is probably under pressure with the start of a business venture, a new house under construction, a new marriage, a newborn baby, a new job, or life in a new country. How does it feel? One of the challenges of modern believers is that, whilst we are blessed with the written testimonies of what the people of faith in the Bible went through, the printed page tempts fast readers to go through these testimonies in seconds, if not minutes. Yet these testimonies took place within time spans of years or decades. We need to learn to be patient in trials whilst giving God glory (Romans 4:20–21), without casting our confidence (Hebrews 10:35–36). Be encouraged and be assured that the current pain is temporal and that you are on the path to a glorious future. With this hope, let's join the apostle Paul in boldly saying, "For **our light and momentary troubles** are achieving for us *an eternal glory* that far outweighs them all" (2 Corinthians 4:17, emphasis mine). Give God the praise!

Prayer

Remember me, O Lord, as I take on the assignments of this life which You have called me to do. Let me not be deterred by their magnitude nor be discouraged by the voices of my enemies. Help me with all needed resources to enable me to stay on course till completion.

Suggested Scriptures for Further Meditation

John 17:4   John 4:34   Psalm 40:7–8

CHAPTER 23

RESILIENCE

Do not gloat over me, my enemy! Though I have
fallen, I will rise. Though I sit in darkness, the Lord
will be my light.

—Micah 7:8

My first experience of winter was in December of 1985 in the
city of London, England, just four months after arriving there
from Accra, Ghana. Dazzled by the display of nature's beautiful
snow falling across the city and beyond, I decided to venture
out of my heated one-bedroom flat to have a feel of the cold
and a touch of the fluffy white snow that had fallen the previous
night. I saw things and learned lessons. I saw people slip and
fall, and being helped by passers-by to get back on their feet.
But what amazed me most was an old woman, probably in her
seventies, who slipped and fell on a pavement after stepping
out of a bus. Without waiting for anyone to help her, she got
back on her feet, smiled at the few people waiting at the bus
stop, and remarked, "Oh, what a lovely day!"

Looking back after many years, I cannot but agree with that
old woman that it was indeed a lovely day. It was a lovely day

not just because of the snow, but also because the old woman demonstrated a tested principle for successful living: the ability to get back on one's feet after a major upset, either in business, career, marriage, or academic pursuit. It was a lovely day for the old woman because, after she fell, she was able to rise up and move on! That attitude or posture is captured in the English word *resilience,* which is our focus in this chapter.

In the corporate world of business, in politics, and in the various disciplines of sports, arts, and entertainment, there are many examples of individuals and corporate bodies (past and present) who bounced back, who managed to stage a successful comeback and regain their titles, their positions, and the glories they had once lost through life's vicissitudes, adversities, trials, and temptations. Where are you today? Are you one of the living "bounced-back" success stories, or you are still lying flat on your back, moaning, groaning, and fretting over your faults, falls, or failures?

It's time to bounce back and join the ranks of those who came back from defeat to win and win again. A few years ago, George Foreman stunned the world of boxing when he bounced back into the ring to regain the heavyweight boxing crown he had lost earlier. Moses failed in his first attempt to fight for the cause of his oppressed brethren in Egypt. Forty years later, he had an encounter with God in the Midian Desert, which enabled him to bounce back to the same palace he had fled from and to accomplish what he had failed to do. When he told Pharaoh, "Let my people go," Moses was speaking with the voice and authority of one who had bounced back. David bounced back to regain his position and title as king of Israel after he had been driven out of office by his own son

Absalom. Peter bounced back after denying the Lord three times before the cock crowed once, to lead the disciples and the church after Christ's resurrection. Job bounced back. But Judas did not bounce back; he got drowned in sorrow, self-pity, and bitterness following his betrayal of the Lord. Judas chose to remain flat on the ground where he fell.

Jesus Christ, our Lord and Saviour, bounced back from the dead. It was impossible for death to keep Him down. You can also be lifted up and placed back on stage, onto the platform of success that God ordained for you before you were conceived in your mum's womb. The ups and downs of this life cannot keep you away from your crown, if you will keep your focus on Him who once proclaimed to a grieving family, "I am the Resurrection and Life." Lazarus bounced back to life as a result of Jesus' intervention (John 11:25–26,43–44). The prodigal son, when he had lost everything and fallen from grace, said, "I will arise and go back to my father" (Luke 15:18,20). He regained his position. You can and will also bounce back. You are resilient! There is elasticity in you!

The Bible quotation heading this chapter echoes the voices of individuals who refused to remain glued to their place of defeat and failure. Tell your enemies, "Though I have fallen, I will rise; though I sit in darkness, the Lord will be my light." Scripture cannot be broken: for though a righteous person falls seven times, he or she rises again. Where have you fallen? Be resilient and get back on your feet.

Prayer

O my enemies, do not gloat over me, for even if I fall, the Lord will raise me up with His outstretched arm and will give me renewed strength and an acceleration to regain lost ground and accomplish my assignment. O Lord, let not my enemies prevail over me.

Suggested Scriptures for Further Meditation

Proverbs 24:16   Psalm 37:23–24   Job 5:17–19

CHAPTER 24

TRAMPLING UPON SERPENTS
AND SCORPIONS

I have given you authority to trample on snakes
and scorpions and to overcome all the power of the
enemy; nothing will harm you.

—Luke 10:19

For any soldier serving in Afghanistan, Somalia, or any of the
war-torn countries of the world, life cannot be taken for granted.
Prior to being taken to serve in these countries, whether as
combat forces or peacekeeping forces, soldiers are given
details about the terrain, the type of enemy forces they will
engage with, the types of weapons used by the enemy forces,
and the enemy's modus operandi. Peacekeeping soldiers
are empowered by international agreements and rules of
engagement. They are armed with weapons designed not only
to defend them but also to neutralize and destroy the opposing
combatants and their weapons. These soldiers know, to a large
extent, the kind of dangers they will be exposed to as long as
they remain on mission.

Every man and woman living in this world is on a mission. To a large extent, our mission field is no different from that of a soldier serving in either Afghanistan or Somalia. We are engaged with enemy forces. There are hidden and sophisticated dangers; there are booby traps, hidden agendas, and hidden snares. For the believer in Christ, the enemy forces are without number; they include principalities, powers, rulers of the darkness of this world, and spiritually wicked people in high places (Ephesians 6:12). Have you seen lately what international peacekeepers patrolling the streets of Kabul or Mogadishu look like? They are in full armour from head to toe. They have embedded in their uniforms sophisticated communication gadgets that enable them to remain in constant contact with their command headquarters in order to receive intelligence information about enemy movements and possible threats.

As believers, we are equally required to put on the whole armour of God so that we may be able to withstand the wiles of the Devil (Ephesians 6:11). We are to be in tune with our Lord through His Word and by praying for intelligence information about the strategies of our enemy forces. It is gratifying to know that our commander-in-chief, the Lord Jesus Christ, knows the terrain, knows the enemy forces, and knows the dangers they pose to us. Therefore, He has made adequate provisions for us. He has given us delegated authority: the right to use power as received and whenever needed to destroy Satan's works. The Lord gives us power over all the power of the Devil. Nothing shall, by any means, hurt us.

"To trample" or "to tread upon" means "to have absolute mastery over." Our commander-in-chief has established the rules of engagement: any encounter between the Devil and a believer shall end in the believer's favour if the believer exercises the authority at his or her disposal. This theme and the assurances of the Lord run throughout Scripture. God is not a person and does not lie. In Psalm 91:1,13, the Lord says that if we abide under His shadow, then we shall tread upon the lion and the adder and trample under our feet the young lion and the dragon (symbols of satanic power). In Psalm 108:13, the Bible assures us that with the help of our God, we shall do mighty acts of valour, for He treads down our foes.

In Psalm 18:36–39, David, the most powerful Old Testament warrior, shares some of the secrets of his wartime successes: "Thou hast enlarged my steps under me that my feet did not slip. I have pursued my enemies, and overtaken them; neither did I turn again till they were consumed. I have wounded them that they were not able to rise; they are fallen under my feet. For thou has girded me with strength unto battle; thou hast subdued under me those that rose up against me." David recognized the source of the power that he had, which enabled him to trample upon his enemies. The Lord knows why He asked the disciples to wait in Jerusalem until they received power from on high; we cannot afford to do without His power. Tap into that power every day to tread upon lions and dragons, to trample upon serpents and scorpions.

"And the God of peace shall bruise Satan under your feet shortly. The grace of our Lord Jesus Christ be with you" (Romans 16:20).

Prayer

Thank You, Lord, that in Your name and through Your death on the cross, we have victory over Satan and his kingdom of demons and darkness. By faith in Your name, I trample upon every serpent and scorpion assigned to act against me by the Devil. Through Your blood and by the word of my testimony, I overcome them all.

Suggested Scriptures for Further Meditation

Luke 10:17   Acts 19:15–16   2 Corinthians 10:3–4

CHAPTER 25

BEAUTY FOR ASHES

And provide for those who grieve in Zion—to bestow
on them a crown of beauty instead of ashes, the oil
of joy instead of mourning and a garment of praise
instead of a spirit of despair.

—Isaiah 61:3

The prophet Isaiah, the son of Amoz, prophesied about Jesus and His ministry on earth more than any other prophet of biblical times. In one of these prophesies, Isaiah 61, Prophet Isaiah spoke about the measure of the anointing of the Holy Spirit upon Jesus and the impact of the Spirit's grace upon Jesus' personality and ministry among people. In His first-ever public reading of the Scriptures in a synagogue in Nazareth, where He was brought up, Jesus read Isaiah 61:1–3 and told the people, "Today this scripture is fulfilled in your hearing" (Luke 4:18–22). In other words, everything Isaiah had prophesied years before was being fulfilled in Jesus, by Jesus, and through Jesus.

Who would doubt and question the measure of the fullness of the Holy Spirit upon Christ's life and ministry? The psalmist

David, was also ahead of his generation with prophetic insight into Jesus' life. David said in Psalm 45:7, "Therefore Your God, has anointed you with oil of gladness above your fellows." With such an overflowing anointing in the Holy Spirit, Jesus exercised—and still, through the church (the body of Christ), exercises—the power of God to preach the gospel of good tidings, to bind up and heal the broken-hearted, to proclaim liberty to the captives and the opening of the prison and of the eyes of those who are bound; to proclaim the acceptable year of the Lord's favour; to comfort all who mourn: "to bestow on them a crown of beauty instead of ashes, the oil of gladness instead of mourning and a garment of praise instead of a spirit of despair" (Isaiah 61:1–3). Praise God for what the anointing by the Spirit through the name of Jesus does to us! I can't help but to repeat: *beauty for ashes, oil of gladness instead of mourning, a garment of praise instead of a spirit of heaviness!*

In Old Testament times, when the people of God were troubled by life's tragedies and humiliating tribulations, they used to express outwardly their inward sorrows by pouring ashes upon their heads and by wearing sackcloth. In such an appearance, a person looks odd and ugly; in such an appearance, a person looks mournful and lacks joy (gladness); in such an appearance, a person becomes so heavily depressed and is unable to sing praises to the Lord. Whom am I talking to? Is it you or someone you know who is broken-hearted and mourning? God in His mercy has made provision, by the Holy Spirit and through the name of Jesus, to minister supernaturally to us when we pass through the straits of pain, deep-seated and bone-deep pain, which cannot be alleviated by analgesics (painkillers) prescribed by a doctor.

We have a great, highly anointed High Priest who has gone through the heavens: Jesus Christ, the Son of God. He not only sympathizes and empathizes with us in our troubled times, but He is also able, through the anointing, the supernatural manifestation of God, to comfort us, heal our bruises, ease our pains, and position us on a Rock that is higher than we, so that we are able to smile at the storm. His anointing, which flows from the throne of God, is able to reach us wherever we are and in whatever situation, to give us stability in turbulent times. God, who cannot lie and swears only by Himself, who is familiar with every human situation, is not insensitive to our needs in difficult times. By His Spirit, God takes away the ashes to restore our beauty; He lifts off our shoulders our sorrows to restore joy; He takes off the spirit of heaviness and clothes us with a garment of praise.

What is beauty, as indicated in the Bible quotation at the start of this chapter? It was said of Hannah in 1 Samuel 1:18 that after she had prayed in Shiloh, *her face was no longer downcast.* The look on her face became one of cheerfulness. A cheerful face is a beautiful face. Your beauty is determined by the look on your face! There is an anointing for cheerfulness, even though we may "walk through the valley of the shadow of death" (Psalm 23:4). May the anointing fall on you to give you *beauty for ashes.*

Prayer

Thank You, O Lord, for Your promise never to leave us or forsake us. You are the Lord who hides us in times of trouble and enables us to triumph over our enemies. You alone can turn our mourning into dancing and our darkness into light. Crown me with beauty, and let Your joy be my strength.

Suggested Scriptures for Further Meditation

Psalm 30:11   Psalm 63:5   Psalm 86:17

CHAPTER 26

DIVINE RESTRAINTS

Paul and his companions traveled throughout the
region of Phrygia and Galatia, having been kept
by the Holy Spirit from preaching the word in the
province of Asia. When they came to the border of
Mysia, they tried to enter Bithynia, but the Spirit of
Jesus would not allow them to.

—Acts 16:6–7

Parenting is one of the most challenging responsibilities in
life. Every responsible parent desires one thing: to guide his
or her child away from what is evil or harmful to what is safe
and beneficial. This is a natural instinct in every parent. It is
therefore not uncommon to see a parent with a young child
(toddler) at home or in a park or church watch closely every
move and action of that boisterous child, lest the child stray
towards a pot of boiling water in the kitchen or try to put into
his or her mouth an unclean object picked up in the park. At
that age, the toddler is too young to discern what is good from
what is harmful. The child therefore needs the support or the
watchful presence of a parent who has the maturity that comes

with age and experience. The child needs a parent with higher and greater intelligence to apply restraints on him or her.

As children of God, we do sometimes act and behave like toddlers: we drift away towards danger because we lack good judgement; we desire certain things, useful, but at the wrong time; we sometimes say the right things, but at inappropriate moments; and so on. We are unable, as it were, to balance what is lawful with what is expedient. Our Father in heaven, who watches over us and who knows the beginning from the end and the end from the beginning, out of His grace and mercy, steps in, through His Word and Spirit, to pull us away from the "boiling water" and to take out of our hand that "filthy object" we are about to put into our mouth; God blinks His eyes at us as a means to caution us not to open that hasty mouth and speak unadvisedly. God applies the brakes of *divine restraint* on us, lest we harm ourselves and bear unnecessary scars on our souls and bodies.

A friend informed me about a write-up that drew a distinction between training children and raising children. Children raised are given only the necessities of life for their physical sustenance. Without training, they end up "killed" by circumstances of life, just as with poultry birds "raised" for the dinner table. When trained, children grow up to survive the vagaries of life and push the frontiers of their family through the generations. God trains us to be responsible sons and daughters.

The psalmist David, cognizant of his frailty in speech, prayed in Psalm 141:3–4, saying, "Set a guard over my mouth, O Lord; keep watch over the door of my lips. Let not my heart be drawn to what is evil, to take part in wicked deeds with men who are evildoers; let me not eat of their delicacies." David was in effect requesting God to impose *divine restraints* on him. His first point of call was his mouth, his lips. I think that my mouth and lips need divine restraint, for "reckless words pierce like a sword, but the tongue of the wise brings healing; truthful lips endure forever but a lying tongue lasts only a moment" (Proverbs 12:18,19). Does your tongue also need *divine restraints?*

The apostle Paul benefited from God's act of supplying *divine restraints* in order for his ministry to the Gentiles to stay on course. In Acts 16:6–10, the Bible records that the Holy Spirit restrained Paul from preaching the Word in the province of Asia; then again, when Paul tried to enter Bithynia, the Holy Spirit did not permit him. Then, by discernment through a vision, Paul got to know the right place to go at the right time. May God divinely restrain us from heading in the wrong direction in life! May God help us to discern between His *divine restraints* and Satan's *diabolical resistance.* We must surrender or yield to God's *divine restraints,* but resist with all our faith and might any type of *diabolical resistance.*

God is good all the time, and all the time God is good. Not only does He restrain us if the need arises, but He also, as a protective Father, imposes *restraints of divine order* on the Devil and evil people who attempt to undermine our progress in life. When Jacob's mean and treacherous uncle Laban pursued him in order to draw Jacob back into servitude and under his control, God, who had earlier urged Jacob to move ahead to his place of destiny, imposed *divine restraints* on Laban so that he would not harm Jacob (Genesis 31:3,24,29). May God lift off our lives any diabolical resistance to our progress. This is our heritage: God's act of providing *divine restraints* is meant for our good. May His will, not ours, be done on earth as it is in heaven. Amen.

Prayer

O Lord, help me comply with Your restraining order to keep me safe from danger. Let those who seek after my life be confounded. Let them stumble and fall. Make their path dark and slippery, and let an angel from Your presence pursue them until they fall into the very trap they have set for me. Restrain them from further acts of aggression against me.

Suggested Scriptures for Further Meditation

Isaiah 30:21   Isaiah 40:4   Isaiah 49:24–25

CHAPTER 27

BREAKING FREE AND MOVING ON

They arrested the apostles and put them in the
public jail. But during the night an angel of the Lord
opened the doors of the jail and brought them out.
"Go, stand in the temple courts," he said, "and tell
the people all about this new life."

—Acts 5:18–20

The book of Acts of the Apostles is a fascinating one. It records
the work of the Holy Spirit among the apostles and believers
of the early church, immediately after the resurrection and
ascension of our Lord and Saviour, Jesus Christ, to heaven.
It is an action-packed book that reveals the power of the Holy
Spirit in the lives of believers who yield to Him and are led by
Him. It captures the truth that the only way by which believers
of today can walk in victory and reign with Christ in this life is
to live by the power of the Holy Spirit. *No Holy Spirit power,
no church. No Holy Spirit power, no victorious Christian living.*

The book of Acts begins with an account of the post-
resurrection life of Christ on earth, during which He requested

the apostles to wait in Jerusalem until they received the promise of the Father. This they did, through *tarrying* or *waiting in prayer,* until the day of Pentecost, when power from on high fell upon them and dwelt within them. A new generation of men and women, boys and girls, filled with power, took over Jerusalem with a message of hope and deliverance, turning upside down the foundation of the lifeless religion practised by the Pharisees and the Sadducees, destroying barriers raised against people's hopes, and obliterating aspirations of the Devil and his kingdom of darkness.

God's presence with the apostles, as evidenced by the indwelling presence of the Holy Spirit, was *too hot for the Devil to handle.* These believers could be neither confined nor contained by the Devil. God's assignment for them on earth was meant to be accomplished. You are just like them; your mission on earth is God-sanctioned and is meant to be accomplished. When you walk in the power of the Holy Spirit, you become *too hot for the Devil to handle.* The Devil may raise opposition against your dream; he may want to keep you under control; he may want to define boundaries for you with the aim of rendering you ineffective and unproductive in your field of duty and assignment. As the above-mentioned Scripture quotation reveals, your enemies, full of jealousy, would love to "put you in jail," to stop you from carrying out your God-given earthly assignment. But they will fail. Again I say, they will fail! They will fail because God wants you to succeed. That is why in the Scripture quoted above we read, "But during the night, an angel of the Lord opened the doors of the jail and brought them out" (Acts 5:19), so that they, *breaking free and moving on,* could carry on with their assignment. It's time to break free, through the power of the Holy Spirit, from every "jail" into which the enemy might have locked you. Angels are on duty to ensure that you are out of every jail of sickness, debt, insecurity, fear, failure, self-pity, anxiety, oppression and depression, isolation, and loneliness—and from the jail of a sense of worthlessness. The Devil is a liar. You are not worthless; you are worthy, for worthy is the Lamb whose blood makes you whole. Break free from the jail and move on to perform and fulfil your assignment.

The angel who released the apostles from the jail said, "Go, stand in the temple courts and tell the people the full message of this new life." That message was not meant to be confined within the walls of a jail; it was meant to be shared wide and far, for the good of many. Your gift, your talent, your dream, your call to duty, your finances, your marriage, your career, the totality of your livelihood, cannot be jailed. We break jail! Change into higher gear and declare war on the Devil's jails. Satan's maximum-security, highly fortified jail is no match for the Holy Spirit. Remember, Jesus said He will build you (His church) and the gates of hell shall not prevail!

The book of Acts ends with the following statement about Paul. I believe it applies to us also. "Boldly and without hindrance, he preached the kingdom and taught about the Lord Jesus Christ" (Acts 28:31). May the power of the Holy Spirit make you bold to move on to accomplish God's purpose for your life.

Prayer

In Jesus' name, I break loose from every orchestration of the Evil One that hinders me from reaching my optimum potential.

I am who God says I am, and no power of darkness can obstruct me henceforth. I am moving ahead into my God-given inheritance.

Suggested Scriptures for Further Meditation

Psalm 35:1–3   Psalm 138:7–8   Isaiah 41:11

CHAPTER 28

SLEEPLESS NIGHTS
IN THE PALACE

That night the king could not sleep; so he ordered the
book of the chronicles, the record of his reign, to be
brought in and read to him. It was found recorded there
that Mordecai had exposed Bigthana and Teresh, two
of the king's officers who guarded the doorway, who
had conspired to assassinate King Xerxes.

—Esther 6:1–2

Certain plights of life are common to all humans, whether
great or small. There are times when we simply cannot sleep,
no matter how comfortable or royal the bed may be. For the
majority of mortals, sleeplessness is an occasional, on-and-
off phenomenon, but for some, it is so chronic that nights of
normal, uninterrupted sleep are paradoxically seen as unusual.
When the human mind is agitated or overwhelmingly occupied
by something, something more often than not related to bad
news or, at times, something associated with good tidings,
sleep—and I mean pleasant, refreshing sleep—is almost
completely lost.

When Ghana lost to Uruguay during the FIFA 2010 World Cup tournament in South Africa, many Ghanaians spent sleepless nights grieving over the loss. Since then, the "hand of Suárez" has become a thorn in the minds of Ghanaian soccer enthusiasts. Luis Suárez was the Uruguayan striker who pulled a goal-bound ball out of his team's net with his hand and thus caused Ghana to lose the quarter-finals. After Ghana had beaten the USA in an earlier match, Ghanaians, for the joy that came with the victory, spent sleepless nights chanting, dancing, and drinking.

Dear friend, do you have good sleep? What is it that has been hampering and disturbing your sleep? Is it unpaid bills, workplace troubles, or a lingering sickness tormenting a loved one? Is it an issue with your boss, husband, or wife? Is it the death of a loved one? In Acts 27, the apostle Paul recounts the ordeal he and other prisoners went through when they travelled by sea on their way to Rome. Given the stormy weather on the sea, they could not sleep for several days. The majority of the people on board could not eat. But having received revelation about God's help in their time of need, Paul stood in the midst of the emotionally shaken and downhearted passengers and exhorted them, saying, "Be of good cheer: for there shall be no loss of any man's life among you" (Acts 27:22–25). Oh, may this same God the apostle served and worshipped, who is also our God, appear in our times of trouble and speak, "Peace, be still!"

It is amazing how God chooses to keep certain records but ignore others. The Bible is silent on sleepless nights in hamlets, but it does focus a great deal on sleepless nights in the palaces of queens and kings. Palaces are seats of power and authority. Decisions made at palaces can make or unmake a person. Whenever God chooses to fight on behalf of His people, He puts pressure on such palaces until favour and help comes to His children. For when the time to favour you, yea, when the set time comes, God shall arise and change the sleeping pattern of kings and queens until they comply and do what God has ordained for you.

When the days of Joseph's exaltation to a high office were near, God interrupted the sleep of Pharaoh one night with strange dreams that required interpretation. No one was found who could interpret the dreams except Joseph. As a result, Joseph was released from prison to become the second most powerful man in Egypt at the time (Genesis 41). After several months and possibly years of Pharaoh's refusal to free Israel from bondage, and in Pharaoh's defiance of Jehovah's request, God chose one night to launch divine, precision-guided missile attacks on Egypt. Thus, He caused sleeplessness in Pharaoh's palace. That same night, Pharaoh surrendered and let the Israelites go (Exodus 12:29–31). Tonight, this week, this month, this year, may God change the sleeping hours of a king because of you, and may you, like Israel, receive your breakthrough.

The Bible says that after the enemies of Daniel succeeded in pushing King Darius to the wall, thus leading the king to put Daniel into the lions' den, King Darius, apparently not pleased with his own decision, went back to his palace. That night, the usual palace music, dance, food, and wine were suspended (Daniel 6:16–23). The king, the Bible says, could not sleep. He fasted. Can you imagine that? He fasted and prayed for Daniel's deliverance. Indeed, God delivered Daniel.

A prayer meeting is going on in the palace of heaven on your behalf. God always makes a way for His people in a crisis. The very night before Haman was to request for the life of Mordecai, the covenant-keeping God was working invisibly, not only to save Mordecai, but also to give him his promotion and honour, which were long overdue. So God caused sleep to pass from King Xerxes, who suddenly became interested in the record books of the kings and so ordered a search into them. The end result of that search led to Mordecai's elevation and to his arch-enemy Haman's humiliation. Mordecai moved from a lower location to a higher location, from being a gatekeeper to becoming the second most powerful man in the land. A night is coming when there will be called an emergency meeting in a palace because of you. By dawn, your income will have multiplied a thousand times, your wardrobe will have changed, your car will have changed, and you will have been relocated to a new address, to a place that really "flows with milk and honey." That night will surely come. Say, "Amen."

Prayer

O Lord God, give no rest to the king or queen who holds the key to my next promotion in life. Let there be no peace in the palace until a royal decree that favours me is issued. I pray in Jesus' name!

Suggested Scriptures for Further Meditation

Psalm 121:3–4   Proverbs 3:25–26   Isaiah 62:6

CHAPTER 29

EYES OPEN, EYES CLOSED, EYES OPEN

And Elisha prayed, "Open his eyes, Lord, so that
he may see." Then the Lord opened the servant's
eyes, and he looked and saw the hills full of horses
and chariots of fire all around Elisha. As the enemy
came down toward him, Elisha prayed to the Lord,
"Strike this army with blindness." So he struck them
with blindness, as Elisha had asked.

—2 Kings 6:17–18

One is not sure what happens in primary schools these days,
but during my time, forty-something years ago, when churches
had unfettered control over mission schools in Ghana, it was a
pleasant feeling to be part of the daily opening morning school
assembly and the closing evening school assembly. These
two school gatherings involving both pupils and teachers were
marked by the singing of good old Spirit-filled hymns and by
the offering of unadulterated prayers. It was not uncommon to
hear a teacher on duty for the day's assembly request pupils
to close their eyes and say or recite the Lord's Prayer, and

request the pupils to open their eyes after reciting it. And, I bet you, so dedicated were pupils and teachers to religious matters that their eyes were tightly closed during prayer sessions and then widely opened when the prayer session was over.

May I ask you to close your eyes for a second? What did you see when you just closed your eyes? Nothing, I guess, because, by closing your eyes, you denied yourself the right and privilege of seeing your surroundings, the world around you. Our eyes, without doubt, are the most important sensory organ in the human body, as they connect us to our physical environment. Without the eyes to see, we are completely cut off from, and severely restricted in our ability to appreciate, the visual beauty of our world. You will appreciate why the blind Bartimaeus (Mark 10:46–52) did not keep quiet when he heard that Jesus was passing by. He shouted louder and louder, saying, "Son of David, have mercy on me." And when Jesus asked Bartimaeus what he wanted Him to do for him, Bartimaeus replied, "Rabbi, I want to see." Jesus restored his sight, his physical sight, so that he could see the physical realm.

But seeing only in the physical realm is not enough for survival in this life. It is much more important for us to also have our eyes spiritually opened so that we can discern spiritual matters, which rule this physical world we live in. Isaiah describes the spiritually blind, the unrepentant sinners who are without Christ, as people who grope along the wall, feeling their way like people without eyes, who at midday stumble as is if it were twilight, and who, among the strong, are like the dead (Isaiah 59:10).

Our Bible quotation for this chapter reveals God's power to control both physical and spiritual eyes. In this context,

God exercises control for the good of his children and all who put their trust in Him. The prophet Elisha's confidence and calmness in the midst of an Aramean threat on his life stemmed from the fact that his spiritual eyes could see God's army around him. On the other hand, the prophet's servant, whose spiritual eyes were unopened, saw only the physical danger around him, not the divine protection around him. When the servant's spiritual eyes were opened through prayer, he saw God's army and his fears vanished into thin air. When our spiritual eyes are open, we fear no evil, for we know where God stands in whatever situation confronts us. We speak like the prophet: "Those who are with us are more than those who are with them" (2 Kings 16:16).

Elisha overcame his enemies on that day, not through the power of machine guns, but by the mighty weapons of God that were at his disposal. Through Elisha's prayer and faith in God, the physical eyes of his enemies were shut and then opened to his advantage. He was therefore able to take charge of the camp of his enemies. What a mighty God we serve! Friend, we live in critical times. Our enemies and the enemies of church are more aggressive than ever and are on a warpath against us. Our eyes must be opened and stay open to discern the movement of God on our behalf so that we don't panic during difficult times, as do people without God.

Prayer

O Lord, let all eyes be blind that seek my destruction, until You bring me to the place of safety and honour which You have prepared for me in this life. Then let the eyes of my enemies see me, with a table set before me in their presence.

Suggested Scriptures for Further Meditation

Psalm 121:5–6   Psalm 16:8   Psalm 25:1–2

CHAPTER 30

LOST AND RESTORED; LOST AND REPLACED

Adam made love to his wife again, and she gave birth to a son and named him Seth, saying, "God has granted me another child in place of Abel, since Cain killed him."

—Genesis 4:25

During the night Abram divided his men to attack them and he routed them, pursuing them as far as Hobah, north of Damascus. He recovered all the goods and brought back his relative Lot and his possessions, together with the women and the other people.

—Genesis 14:15–16

Truly speaking, the fifteenth chapter of the gospel according to Saint Luke can be referred to as the chapter of the parable of the lost. In this chapter, Jesus taught three parables to explain the opportunity God has created for the salvation of every lost soul: the parable of the lost sheep, the parable of the lost coin, and the parable of the lost son. Jesus ended each parable on a familiar note, mentioning the joy that came with the recovery of a precious asset that had been lost. It reminds me of the joy I once had in Sydney, Australia, when a camera I had misplaced in a shopping mall was found and returned to me intact. I was on cloud nine! Tell me your story about "lost and found." I hope you are forever grateful to God for His help.

Abraham was forever grateful to God for helping him recover all the goods and to bring back his nephew Lot and his possessions when the latter was captured during a time of war. After David had cried over the loss of his wives, children, and goods to the raiding Amalekites, he, the Bible tells us, found strength in the Lord, regained his composure, pursued the Amalekites, and overpowered them. David *recovered* everything the Amalekites had taken, including his two wives (1 Samuel 30). When the axe-head fell into the river Jordan, a cry was made to the prophet Elisha by one of his student prophets (2 Kings 6:1–7). The man of God asked, "Where did it fall?" An axe-head represents one's strength, competence, expertise, and competitive advantage. Has your axe-head fallen into the deep? Have you lost ground to your rival, your competitor? Hear this and hear it by faith: you will recover your axe-head. By the power of God, the prophet caused the axe-head to float on the river surface, after which it was recovered. Yes, in this life, God has made provision for us to recover certain precious lost valuables. We can't afford losing all the time. It is time to take back what the Devil has taken away. "Seek and ye shall find" is the assurance the Son of God gives us. Yes, all recoverable things must be recovered.

But we also need to understand—and praise God that the Bible teaches so—that some other things, when lost, cannot be recovered; they can only be *replaced.* Bless your soul! Jehovah Jireh, El-Shaddai, the many-breasted God, has made provision for the replacement of certain lost valuables. In Genesis 4:25, the Bible tells us that God gave Adam and Eve a son called Seth to replace Abel, whom his brother Cain had killed! God knows how to compensate for losses. Has your Abel (a loved one) gone to be with the Lord? Have you lost your job, or has your car been stolen or smashed beyond repair? Have you lost a fiancée or fiancé to another person? Have you lost some money? All these circumstances are heart-breaking. I pray to God to bring about a replacement. He has done it before, and He can do it again.

Do you remember Job? After Satan went on a rampage, destroying Job's business and properties and killing his children and servants, Job did not recover any of these. He learned to let go, trusting God. But listen, dear one: the Lord, the Bible says, blessed the latter part of Job's life more than the first! God *replaced* everything Satan destroyed: sheep, camels, yoke of oxen, and donkeys. God replaced Job's lost children with new ones: seven sons and three beautiful daughters (Job 42:12–17). When Satan took away Judas Iscariot from the Twelve, God brought Matthias as replacement (Acts 1:26). God can replace a lost bicycle with a car! So stop crying, cursing, crawling, and complaining in bitterness over your loss. If God does not recover it for you, then you can be sure He will replace it. Whichever way, you win and Satan loses.

Prayer

Lord Jesus, restore unto me the years that the Enemy has taken away. Restore unto me the lost opportunities. As replacement for the treasures and trophies that I have lost, grant me treasures and trophies that are more glorious.

Suggested Scriptures for Further Meditation

Jeremiah 30:17   Isaiah 30:26   Joel 2:25

CHAPTER 31

THE LORD, MIGHTY IN BATTLE

The Lord your God is with you, the Mighty Warrior
who saves. He will take great delight in you; in his
love he will no longer rebuke you, but will rejoice
over you with singing.

—Zephaniah 3:17

What an amazing truth! The Lord God is mighty in battle!
But why would God fight? Whom is God fighting against?
Or rather, we may ask, whom is God fighting for? In this life,
there are battles. Some are avoidable; others are unavoidable.
Some are protracted; others are short-lived. There are battles
fought in the physical realm, whilst others are fought in the
spiritual realm. All battles, irrespective of the type, are costly:
lives are lost or maimed; properties are lost or destroyed. A
dictionary's definition of the word *battle* will help us understand
the magnitude of what we are talking about. As a noun, the
word *battle* has at least two meanings. First, it means an "armed
fight," which is a large-scale combat between armies, with
warships and aircraft. Second, it means "struggle," a drawn-
out conflict between adversaries or against powerful forces.

Ever since Satan led a rebellion in heaven against the authority of God and was thrown out of heaven together with his legions of fallen angels, armed fight and struggle have been inseparable from our very existence on this planet and beyond. In Genesis 4, it was a struggle between Cain and Abel. In Genesis 13, it was struggle for green pastures between Abraham's herdsmen and Lot's herdsmen. In Genesis 27, it was a struggle between Esau and Jacob. In 2 Samuel 3:1, it was a struggle between the House of David and the House of Saul. In the books of Daniel (chapter 10) and Revelation (chapter 12), we find the archangel Michael engaged in battles against the prince of Persia and the Dragon in the heavenly realms. The apostle Paul did not mince words when he said, "For our struggle is not against flesh and blood, but against rulers ... against the spiritual forces of evil in the heavenly realms" (Ephesians 6:12).

Where has life's battle line been drawn against you? And where does God stand in all these conflicts? The Lord God, who is mighty in battle, does not stand aloof. He takes sides; He is either on your side or on the other side. When it comes to battles, God has a pedigree. As a covenant-keeping God, He knows His obligations to His blood-bought children, of whom you are an integral part. He knows you by name, and it is about time you also knew Him by name. He is Jehovah Sabbaoth (Lord of Hosts), translated as "Lord Almighty"; this is the name David used when he challenged Goliath (1 Samuel 17:45). Stated in another way, Jehovah Sabbaoth is the commander-in-chief of the heavenly armies. He is in complete command and in total control. There is no troop movement, so to speak, anywhere in heaven or earth of which He is unaware. God can fight on land, on sea, in the air, and under the earth. Where is the battle raging on in your life?

In Exodus 14:14, Israel was assured, "The Lord will fight for you; you need only to be still." One of the strategies of spiritual warfare I gleaned from Israel's exodus from Egypt, and indeed the final strategy by which the enemy was dealt a devastating blow, was "standing still." The Bible puts it this way, in Exodus 14:13: "And Moses said unto the people, 'Fear ye not, *stand still*, and see the salvation of the Lord, which he will show to you today: for the Egyptians whom ye have seen today, ye shall see them again no more forever.'" To cast fear aside and stand still in earnest expectation of the Lord, it has to be in our spirit and the marrow of our bones that the Lord is not just *mighty,* but the *Almighty.* And with that, we shall surely "see the salvation of the Lord." In Exodus 23:27, God assured His people, "I will send my terror ahead of you and throw into confusion every nation you encounter. I will make all your enemies turn their backs and run." In Deuteronomy 20:4, Moses tells you and me, "For the Lord your God is the one who goes with you to fight for you against your enemies to give you victory." And when King Jehoshaphat of Judah, confronted in battle by a vast Moabite/Ammonite army, turned to the Lord of Hosts for help, he received this word of prophesy: "Do not be afraid nor be discouraged by this vast army, for the battle is not yours, but God's" (2 Chronicles 20:15). I love what Hezekiah told his people at the time when Sennacherib, king of Assyria, was beating war drums against Judah: "Be strong and courageous... for there is greater power with us than with him. With him is only the arm of flesh, but with us is the Lord our God to help us and to fight our battles" (2 Chronicles

32:7,8). Glory be to God! In the face of all our battles, let us join the apostle Paul and declare boldly, "We are more than conquerors through Him who loved us."

Prayer

O God of the heavenly armies, may Your presence go ahead of me to rout out those who fight against me. Lord, do not withdraw Your mighty sword until the camp of my enemies is no more.

Suggested Scriptures for Further Meditation

Genesis 49:24   Psalm 24:8   Deuteronomy 3:24

CHAPTER 32

GOD REMEMBERS

> But God remembered Noah and all the wild animals
> and the livestock that were with him in the ark,
> and he sent a wind over the earth, and the waters
> receded.
>
> —Genesis 8:1

In the league table listing the most favourite given Christian names worldwide, one is not likely to find the name Zechariah. But a number of individuals, the majority of them in the Old Testament, were called by that name: Zechariah, king of Israel, son of Jeroboam (2 Kings 14:29); and Zechariah, son of Jehoiada the high priest, who was murdered for prophesying against King Joash (2 Chronicles 24:20–21). In one of his most fiery denunciations of the Pharisees and the Scribes, Jesus made reference to this murder (Matthew 23:35). Then we also have Zechariah, a prophet, who inspired the Jews to rebuild the temple during the days of King Darius (Ezra 5:1; Zechariah 7:1). Last but not the least was Zechariah the high priest, the father of John the Baptist and husband of Elizabeth (Luke 1:5).

If I could have the opportunity to return to my mum's womb and be born afresh, I think I would go for the name Zechariah, for the simple reason of what that name means: "God has remembered." What would life on earth have been like if God was mercilessly forgetful and not graciously remembering? God, the tested and tried, remembers! Throughout the Bible, the expression "and God remembered" is almost always followed by God's divine act of showing mercy and extending unusual favour towards an individual or group of people who had been in dire straits, in a difficult overwhelming situation that could be solved by neither human wisdom nor human ability. God simply came down to remove the individual or people from an excruciating situation. Being the changeless God, He still does this!

Come with me and see for yourself God's track record. Who else can compare with Him (Isaiah 44:8)? For Noah, it was a messy torrent of floodwaters that kept him and his family confined in an ark for months. I imagine that food was running out and that the sewage system in the ark was overstretched. When the Enemy (Satan) comes like a flood, God raises the Holy Spirit as a standard against him! *God remembered* Noah and sent a wind across the earth to dry up the floodwaters. Noah and his family were able to come out to start life afresh. God will remember you also; your days of confinement to any sickening situation are over.

God remembered Abraham's intercession for Lot, so He sent angels to Sodom and Gomorrah to rescue Lot and his family before the fire fell on those cities (Genesis 19:29). Rachel had been married for years without children. When *God remembered* her, her womb was opened. She conceived and brought forth a son, Joseph, and said, "God has taken away my disgrace" (Genesis 30:22–24). Help is coming your way. You'll not be disgraced! Hear Hannah, one of my most favourite personalities in the Bible, share her testimony. Hannah was barren, without children, and was mocked and laughed at by her rival woman in marriage who had children. Hannah cried to God, and the *Lord remembered* her; she conceived and brought forth Samuel (1 Samuel 1:19–20)! Hannah composed a song in which she praised the Lord, saying, "He raises the poor from the dust and lifts the needy from the ash heap; He seats them with princes and has them inherit a throne of honour" (1 Samuel 2:8). Glory! Glory! You will inherit your throne of honour!

As a covenant-keeping God, He remembers. In expressing his thanks to God, the psalmist of Psalm 136:23 declares, "To the One who *remembered* us in our low estate His love endures forever." When Samson saw himself humiliated and brought lower than minus zero by his enemies, the Philistines, he did the most appropriate thing: he called on the God who remembers. Hear Samson pray to God in Judges 16:28: "O Sovereign Lord, *remember me.* O God, please strengthen me just one more, and let me with one blow get revenge on the Philistines for my two eyes." God remembered Samson. The amazing twist is that God does not remember our sins if we confess and forsake them; instead, He remembers our good works and our labour of love. He will remember you also. Amen.

Prayer

You are the God who remembered Noah, so remember me.
You are the God who remembered Sarah, so remember me.
You are the God who remembered Rachel, so remember me.
You are the God who remembered Israel in its time of distress,
so remember me.

Suggested Scriptures for Further Meditation

Genesis 30:22   Exodus 2:24–25   Psalm 115:12

CHAPTER 33

THE MIRROR

Do not merely listen to the word, and so deceive yourselves. Do what it says. Anyone who listens to the word but does not do what it says is like a man who looks at his face in a mirror and, after looking at himself, goes away and immediately forgets what he looks like.

—James 1:22–24

One of the most common and useful devices ever in the possession of humanity is the mirror. Its power to reflect light, images of people, living things, and objects that are placed in front of it is among the most fascinating phenomena of all time. Mirrors are in many places: homes, hotels, offices, shops and other business concerns, highways and street corners, motor vehicles, submarines, and women's handbags and purses. They come in various shapes, forms, and sizes. Depending on the type, size, and use, a mirror may be cheap or expensive.

No person who values his or her public appearance ever leaves home without first looking into the mirror. When we stand in front of the mirror before we check into the public domain, it as if we are seeking its opinion of our appearance. More often than not, the mirror comes out as a good judge: the necktie or headscarf is out of shape and therefore needs adjustment, or the foundation makeup is too loud and scary for a Sunday Communion service or an important interview. The driving mirrors fixed at select points in a standard motor vehicle enable the driver to locate other motorists behind him or her and on his or her side; without the mirrors, making a turnaround or joining another lane on the highway could result in a serious accident. Unfortunately, on the highways in some developing countries, there are commercial vehicles without driving mirrors. What a risk to life and property!

There are well-fabricated and badly fabricated domestic mirrors. In front of a good mirror, one sees the exact image of himself or herself in terms of shape, size, and height. Bad mirrors, however, give a distorted image of a person, such as an enlarged head, diminished or extended height, and, at worst, a bloated face reminiscent of a badly beaten boxer who has been knocked out in a match. It is therefore important to look at oneself in a good mirror in order to have the right reflection of oneself.

The images we carry about ourselves are influenced not only by the mirrors we look into, but also, much more important, by the words we hear, by our perceptions, and by the experiences we go through in life. What is your real image? Gideon in the Bible (Judges 6) had a terrible, terrifying, and tormenting image of himself. At that time, Israel was under the oppressive Midianite regime. According to Gideon, his clan was the weakest in Manasseh and he was the least in his family. What a tragic image Gideon apportioned to himself!

Many of the Israelites who left Egypt, bound for the Promised Land, did not make it. Through fear and unbelief fueled by evil words they heard from unbelieving reporters, they exchanged their God-given image as possessors of Canaan for the image of grasshoppers (Numbers 13:33). The image you carry of yourself largely determines your chances of reaching your goal in life. Our self-image is a reflection of our mindset.

What did God do to turn Gideon around, from his "weakest and least" mindset and image into the "mighty warrior" image, the image that enabled him, with an army of three hundred, to defeat the Midianite army consisting of hundreds of thousands soldiers? God spoke into Gideon's hearing and spirit, saying that he was neither weak nor least, but rather bold and strong. This brought about a revolutionary change to Gideon's burned-out mindset. When God took Gideon by his hand and made him look intently into the mirror of God's Word of perfect liberty, Gideon saw his real, God-approved image, not the distorted image imposed on him by the tyrannical rule of the Midianites and by wobbly words spoken, perhaps, in his family home and neighbourhood. In order words, God restored Gideon's sense of self-worth by speaking appropriate words at the appropriate time.

When you stand in front of a mirror, what do you see? Do you see yourself as one redeemed by Christ's blood and set apart by the Spirit as an ambassador for God's kingdom? Do you see yourself as one highly favoured and of the royal priesthood, ordained with delegated authority and power of the Lord Jesus to bind and to loose, and to trample upon serpents and scorpions? Do you see yourself adorned with the full armour of God and living by faith, not by sight, with your unveiled face reflecting the Lord's glory and being transformed into His likeness with ever-increasing glory? What do you see? Come on, put on your real image, as recreated by God in Christ Jesus. Take God at His Word, and live by His promises. In Isaiah 52:1, God calls on Jerusalem, saying, "Awake, awake, O Zion, clothe yourself with strength. Put on your garments of splendor, O Jerusalem, the holy city." What kind of image have you clothed yourself with? The best mirror you can look into is God's Word, in which God tells you who you are, what you can do, and what you can become. That's the perfect mirror. Christ Jesus is the Word of God. In Christ, we discover our real self, a true reflection of God's image, which He deposited in us at creation. In Him, what was distorted through Adam's disobedience is restored. Our daily fellowship with the Lord Jesus, through the Word of God, allows God's image of righteousness, purity, and holiness to be seen in us. Look into God's Word daily, and carry the right image of yourself. In this, we find true fulfillment in life.

Prayer

Thank You, Lord Jesus, for Your redemptive work, which has restored me as I was created in the image of God. I demolish every negative word that has ever been hurled at me by anyone. I pull down any unproductive thought I have ever entertained in my mind. I renounce all negative words I have ever uttered against myself. I renew my mindset in the light of Your Word, and I accept who I am in You, Lord Jesus.

Suggested Scriptures for Further Meditation

Psalm 139:14   Ephesians 2:10   Philippians 1:6

CHAPTER 34

WHEN JESUS PASSES BY

How God anointed Jesus of Nazareth with the Holy
Spirit and power, and how he went around doing
good and healing all who were under the power of
the devil, because God was with him.

—Acts 10:38 (NIV)

Have you ever asked yourself how many TV camera operators
and paparazzi would have followed Jesus on His many
seemingly endless missionary treks during His life on earth
over two millennia ago, considering the uncommon miracles
that accompanied His teachings and preaching? Imagine how
CNN, Sky TV, BBC, ABC, or any of the world's major twenty-
four-hour TV channels would have reported the miracle that
happened at the wedding in Cana where He turned water into
wine; His feeding of five thousand men, in addition to women
and children, with five loaves of bread and two fishes; His
raising from the dead of Jairus' daughter; and His walking on
the sea. Tell me, how would CNN have reported the raising of
Lazarus four days after being dead and buried? Your guess is
as good as mine.

Breaking news! Jesus has done it again. This time, He has brought back to life a man named Lazarus who had been buried for four days. We now go over live to our chief correspondent, who is standing among the teeming, bewildered crowd in the graveyard with Lazarus. Meanwhile, Jesus, we are told, has left the scene with His disciples and is on His way to Jericho.

And we all know what happened when Jesus entered Jericho: a blind man named Bartimaeus sat along the street, begging for alms. When he heard that *Jesus was passing by,* he shouted, "Jesus, Son of David, have mercy on me." Once Jesus heard Bartimaeus' cry, what followed was another example of breaking news: Bartimaeus' eyes were opened, and his life was never the same again. Jesus relocated him. Also, the title "blind beggar," which Bartimaeus had carried all his life, was cancelled forever by the power of Jesus. May He cancel anything negative in your life.

Lest you begin to tell yourself that all these events are history, be ye informed that Jesus Christ, King of Kings and Lord of Lords, is still passing by. No community is too poor or too rich to scare Him off. The risen Lord has not changed His itinerary: by His Spirit and power, He is still going around doing good and healing all who are under the power of the Devil. He knows the address of people in distress and reaches out to help them. The Bible says He crossed over the Sea of Galilee and went into the region of Gerasenes, where He was met by a man who was naked and had been driven away from human dwellings by the forces of evil, a man who spent his days and nights in a cemetery, cutting himself with sharp stones, crying, and acting like a wild animal (Mark 5:1–20). When a human being is treated that way by the cruelty of Satan, families and society give up on that person. But I tell you, Jesus does not. He will go to any length to show mercy and to do good to the oppressed. Jesus confronted the forces of evil and set the man free. That man became a great evangelist: breaking news! I tell you, Jesus is still passing by to turn people's mourning into dancing.

Unlike the breaking news on major international TV channels, which more often than not centres on deaths, wars, scandals, earthquakes, and tsunamis, Jesus' breaking news is good news. It is always about Jesus' forgiving a sinner, healing the sick and afflicted, setting captives free, imparting anointing upon someone, opening doors, and making a way where there is no way. It is all about Jesus' healing broken lives and shattered relationships, putting smiles on people's faces, giving comfort to people in times of sorrow, giving businesses a much-needed push, opening wombs that are closed, and leading people into lasting marital homes. It's all about Jesus' giving assurances to worried mums and dads that their prodigal sons and daughters will return home repentant. It is about His telling you, "Be of good cheer." Trust Him to pass by your way this week with His kind of breaking news, which brings real joy!

Prayer

I am Your portion, O God, so do not pass me. Turn Your gracious attention on me and do me good. Let the next breaking news be about me, that God has heard my cry and has put a smile on my face and a new song on my tongue. To You alone be the glory.

Suggested Scriptures for Further Meditation

Mark 1:32–34   Mark 5:34   Acts 10:38

CHAPTER 35

GREAT CLOUD OF WITNESSES

> Therefore, since we are surrounded by such a great
> cloud of witnesses, let us throw off everything that
> hinders and the sin that so easily entangles. And
> let us run with perseverance the race marked out
> for us.
>
> —Hebrews 12:1

The word *witness,* in the form of a noun, almost always stirs up the image of a courtroom scene, where a person or group of people appear in the dock (or the witness stand) to give testimony about what they knew, heard, or saw when the defendant(s) allegedly committed an act against the law. By the testimony of a witness or witnesses, an accused person may be condemned or set free. So crucial is the role of an eyewitness that in the ninth of the Ten Commandments, God warns, "You shall not give false testimony against your neighbour" (Exodus 20:16). The testimony of witnesses is required to establish truth in any matter (Deuteronomy 19:15).

How important, therefore, it is to be a truthful witness or to have truthful witnesses testifying in a matter for our sake!

Our focus in this chapter, however, is not about witnesses in a courtroom, but rather about witnesses to the Christian faith who testify to the abundant life Christ Jesus gives; the life of faith in the living God for whom all the people mentioned in Hebrews 11 lived and died; and the same life of faith to which we have been called—that faith whose author and finisher is the Lord Jesus Christ Himself. He has not prescribed for us a life with which He is unfamiliar, one that is unreal. He came to this world to live a life of faith with total dependence on God. By His unwavering commitment to His Father, Jesus triumphed over Satan, sin, and all evil, bearing testimony to the fact that a life lived in obedience to God's will is a life characterized by victory over all circumstances in this sin-stained world.

Jesus is our first-most witness to the Christian faith. In this sense, in the book of Revelation, He is called *the faithful witness* (Revelation 1:5). If He lives and abides in us, then we have what it takes to overcome and reign in this life. As the faithful witness to the righteous, faith-filled life to which God has called us, Jesus assures us, "Because I live, you will live also" (John 14:19). Hear Him say it again, in another way: "Just as the living Father sent me and I live because of the Father, so the one who feeds on me will live because of me" (John 6:57).

What other guarantees do we need from Him in order to walk confidently in this life? He came as God's manifestation to destroy the works of the Devil, so that in Him and through Him alone we would have dominion over the Devil and sin (1 John 3:8). Sin hinders. You know that the name *Satan* means "the opposer"; thus, Satan and sin have one thing in common: *hindrance*. But through His blood, Jesus has provided the basis for us to exercise dominion over both Satan and sin on a daily basis! Hallelujah! So, like Him, we should be bold enough to tell Satan and sin, "Get behind us!" We should hold on to the faith for which the heroes and heroines of faith in Hebrews 11—and many others, including those in contemporary times and you— once contended for and still do contend, looking unto Christ, in whom we live, move, and have our being.

The challenges you face today were once faced by some in the cloud of witnesses who, through faith, overcame those challenges. Their lives bear testimony to the fact that you will also overcome. They are, as it were, cheering you on from the grandstand of life's amphitheatre to press on and not give up. So as we look at these men and women, there should come to our minds this conviction: that the God of yesterday is also the God of today. In other words, the things that God did through Enoch, Noah, and Abraham, through Jacob, Isaac, Joseph, Moses, and Rahab, He is able to do today, through you and through me! May the life we live today bear testimony to the fact that we are witnesses to God's saving grace and power. One amazing truth to encourage you about the lives of these heroes of faith is that none of them was spared challenges. Don't look only at their victories and testimonies. In looking at their challenges, you will realize that you are on course despite your challenges. Amen!

Prayer

Lord Jesus, help my faith and cause me to tread the path of faith upon which the heroes and heroines of Hebrews 11 once walked. Allow me to share in the victory and the crown they received from You. Cause me to live by faith and not by sight, simply trusting You every day, as long as life shall last.

Suggested Scriptures for Further Meditation

Isaiah 43:10   Acts 1:8   Revelation 1:5

CHAPTER 36

STARTING AFRESH

The Lord said to Moses, "Chisel out two stone tablets like the first ones, and I will write on them the words that were on the first tablets, which you broke. Be ready in the morning, and then come up on Mount Sinai. Present yourself to me there on top of the mountain."

—Exodus 34:1–2

How refreshing it is to know that in this life, God, our Creator, knows that we are all fallible. He gives us, and I mean every one of us, opportunities to begin afresh on an assignment, task, project, or mission that we had previously attempted to execute but failed miserably with. Do you know that God's hall of fame bears the names of men and women who once failed before succeeding at long last? Great men and women like Moses, Joshua, Ruth, David, Jonah, Peter, and others once upon a time failed, once upon a time had their dreams shattered. In the lives of these ancient people and of many more in our contemporary times, there were moments of failure, but the grace of God created rooms for them to reorganize, strategize anew, and start afresh the same task or assignment they had previously fumbled at doing. Praise God that they were able to turn their fields of failure and defeat into fields of success and victory. A characteristic feature of such men and women is that they took responsibility for their failures—a sign of humility—and this provoked God to lift them up to heights of success.

At the foot of Mount Sinai, Moses flared up in anger at the rebellious behavior of Israel. He lost control of himself and smashed into pieces the two tablets of stone inscribed with the first-ever commandments, handwritten by God Himself (Exodus 32:19). Yes, like Moses, some of us allowed people to provoke us into uncontrollable anger, and so we lost control of the steering wheel and crashed our efforts to do what God had commissioned us to do. Was that the end of Moses? No. God gave him another chance, as recorded in the Bible quotation above. Listen to what God said to Moses: "Chisel out two stone tablets like the first ones, and I will write on them the words that were on the first tablets, which you broke." God asked him to get two new stones for the task to be done again. This time, it must be well done. The written laws must get to the people intact. And so it was. And so it ought to be with your next attempt. You broke it the other time(s), but you won't break it this time!

David's first attempt at getting the ark of the covenant back to Judah, after years of the ark's being held captive by the Philistines, ended in disaster, as one person died in the process (1 Chronicles 13:7–12). David's problem was that he had the zeal to carry out that task but lacked the prescribed knowledge for transporting the ark. Still, David did not allow the dream of getting the ark back to Jerusalem die. He humbled himself by acknowledging his mistake, and God created another chance for him. The next time, David got it right and brought the ark into Jerusalem (1 Chronicles 15:1–15). Where have you abandoned your "ark"? Are you still grieving over your mistakes and your failure to bring it before? Start afresh; God will help you.

If you are a "pebble" like Simon Peter, unstable and prone to failures, I assure you that God's manifold grace and uncommon mercy can transform you into stable rock – Cephas - adorned with power to succeed where you failed. Simon Peter is the man who, before the cock crowed once, denied his Master three times. You know why he failed? He failed because he put confidence in the flesh (self). But upon repenting and accepting responsibility for his abysmal performance, Peter was restored by the Lord, who handed over to him the mantle of leadership of the church in Jerusalem. This same Peter, on the day of Pentecost, preached the gospel of Jesus Christ, after which three thousand souls accepted Christ. You are not a failure. What has happened to you is not uncommon to heroes. Lift up your eyes to the Lord. His grace is sufficient to carry you through to victory. Start afresh.

Prayer

O Lord Jesus, renew my strength to start afresh and to continue from where I left off on my assignment and dream. May Your presence carry me through to a glorious end.

Suggested Scriptures for Further Meditation

Psalm 51:12–13   Psalm 37:23–24   Proverbs 24:16

CHAPTER 37

START TO FINISH

I have fought the good fight, I have finished the race,
I have kept the faith.

—2 Timothy 4:7

The season for international athletics always comes with surprises. Some famous athletes make the headlines with great regularity; some otherwise unknown athletes break into the limelight. Flags of the winning athletes' nations fly at full mast; lights flash across stadiums with the click of camera buttons as fans and spectators yearn to take the best shot of their heroes and heroines who finish a field or track event on a high note. For each track-and-field event, there is a governing rule with which an athlete must comply if he or she wants to receive the victor's crown or prize. So in the track events, it's not just who is first to cross the finish line that decides the winner; it is who observes the rules that underpin the particular race. According to 2 Timothy 2:5, "Similarly, if anyone competes as an athlete, he does not receive the victor's crown unless he competes according to the rules." There are many forms of track events: short-distance races such as the 100 metre and

200 metre, and long-distance races such as the 5,000 metre and 10,000 metre. Professional athletes are trained in the art of running each type of race. Have you observed the shape, size, and weight of these athletes? Have you also taken note of the uniforms they wear to compete? Their diets and lifestyles, before, during and after the athletic season, are subject to disciplinary regimes to ensure that anytime, anywhere, they are fit to start the race and finish in good time (1 Corinthians 9:24–27). Celebrated athletes have all learned to throw off everything that hinders and easily entangles them so that they can run with perseverance the race that is marked out for them (Hebrews 12:1).

Some athletes start a race but never finish; they quit halfway through the event. Such athletes are in the news for the wrong reason. How important is it to start and finish your race? The apostle Paul relates our mission on earth, our call to the faith, our call to duty, to a race. Jesus stressed the importance of paying the cost of discipleship in order to finish the race of the Christian call. This is how Jesus put it in Luke 14:28–29: "Suppose one of you wants to build a tower. Will he not first sit down to estimate the cost to see if he has enough money to complete it? For if he lays the foundation, and is unable to finish, everyone who sees it will ridicule him, saying, 'This fellow *began* to build and was not able to *finish.*'"

So I charge you by the mercies of God to join the "start and finish" club. The membership of this club includes noble men and women. God, our heavenly Father and the Creator of heaven and earth, took six days to complete His creation. Noah started to build the ark when he was commanded by God; 120 years later, he finished it. Caleb and Joshua started in Egypt and finished in the Promised Land. They defied the rough desert life and the rugged terrain and marched on to the finishing line in milk-and-honey Canaan. Jesus, our Lord and Saviour, started in a manger in the little town of Bethlehem. Thirty-three years later, on Calvary's cross, He declared triumphantly, "It is finished." It is our turn—and we dare not fail.

"Brothers, I do not consider myself yet to have taken hold of it. But one thing I do: Forgetting what is behind and straining towards what is ahead, I press on towards the goal to win the prize for which God has called me heavenward in Christ Jesus" (Philippians 3:13–14).

Prayer

Lord Jesus, author and finisher of my faith, teach me how to press on to a place of excellence and distinction until I have accomplished Your purpose for my life.

Suggested Scriptures for Further Meditation

Nehemiah 6:15–16   Ecclesiastes 7:8   2 Corinthians 8:11

CHAPTER 38

SHOWERS TO REFRESH THE WEARY

You gave abundant showers, O God; you refreshed
your weary inheritance.

—Psalm 68:9

In a long-distance race, such as the ten thousand metre or the marathon at the Olympics, when 75 per cent of the distance has been covered—that is, as the race enters into the last quarter to the finishing line—the die is cast and the difference between men and boys, women and girls, the strong and weak, begins to emerge. In the last quarter of the race, stamina is the key. Athletes who have developed stamina begin to draw on that strength to run faster, with their eyes set on the prize and the crown meant for those who endure to the end.

How do you feel, or how do you see yourself, at this time of the year? Tired, sleepy, exhausted, drained, somnolent, drowsy, worn out, wiped out, shattered, disillusioned? Do you see yourself stronger today than you were a few months or years ago? In the last quarter, as in a marathon, weariness begins to set in and athletes reach for water placed along the sides of the track to replenish the water lost through excessive sweating. They do this in order to maintain the critical mass of water the body needs to complete the race.

Where are you in your journey of life? Well done, but the journey is not yet over. Praise God for His help so far, but you still need His help to reach the journey's end. You don't want to finish the race crownless. "Run to win" was Paul's admonition to the Corinthians. We want to be among those who satisfy the criteria for winning bronze, silver, and gold medals. That's why, like athletes running the last quarter, we also need to reach for the much-needed water from the divine showers and springs of God that refresh the weary so that we run the race victoriously and with the stamina of champions, moving to higher ground with a greater allocation of life's best. God will pour on us abundant showers for a glorious finish and will lead us beside living springs to refresh our souls with new strength and determination to pursue life's best as defined by Him, our Maker. Shout a loud amen.

His promises are still alive with vigor, and we want to steadfastly stand in them. In the Scripture quotation above, the psalmist proclaims, "You gave abundant showers, O God; you refreshed your weary inheritance." Are you weary? There is enough refreshment for you. Isaiah says, "God gives strength to the weary and increases the power of the weak" (Isaiah 40:29). And as you hold onto the hope you have had all this while, God will surely visit you with fresh showers to cause that dream He breathed into your spirit some time ago to come true. You will experience refreshment in your innermost being and be energized by that hope you have in God, for those who keep that hope, according to Isaiah, "will renew their strength.

They will soar on wings like eagles; they will run and not grow weary, they will walk and not be faint."

The prophet Elijah, wearied by the threats of Jezebel, wished he were dead. Do not be wearied by any threatening situation. Do not be drained of joy if the miracle you have believed that God would perform has not yet happened. God is not moved by deadlines; He makes all things beautiful in His time. But He does not leave us alone in our moments of exhaustion. He refreshes us. So for Elijah, an angel sent by God touched him and said, "Get up and eat, for the journey is too much for you." I tell you, God knows how far you have come and how close you are to your breakthrough. And what did Elijah do? He got up and ate and drank. That's refreshment. Strengthened, he travelled forty days and forty nights until he reached Horeb, the mountain of God (1 Kings 19:3–9).

Cheer up, friend. Be refreshed by the grace and mercy of God. You, too, will reach your mountain; you will end on your way up, not down. Be refreshed, all ye who are weary, for the living springs of God have not dried up.

Prayer

I need Your showers, O Lord, Your showers of blessing that refresh the weary, lest my enemies jubilate over my plight. Lead me beside Your springs of life so I may remain refreshed and fruitful in every good work. Like Jacob, I hold on. I will not let You go, O Lord, until You bless me.

Suggested Scriptures for Further Meditation

Zechariah 10:1   Isaiah 44:3   Ezekiel 34:26

CHAPTER 39

WORSHIPPING GOD WITHOUT RESERVATION

> Then Pharaoh summoned Moses and said, "Go, worship the Lord. Even your women and children may go with you; only leave your flocks and herds behind." But Moses said, "You must allow us to have sacrifices and burnt offerings to present to the Lord our God. Our livestock too must go with us; not a hoof is to be left behind."
>
> —Exodus 10:24–26

The exodus of the descendants of Abraham from Egypt to the Promised Land was with excitement, but not without struggle. Pharaoh put up a fierce resistance, refusing to let the Israelites go so that they might hold a festival or worship service for the Lord in the wilderness. Several thousands of years later, in our twenty-first century AD, "Pharaoh"—Satan—still puts up relentless resistance to any attempt by the believer in Christ to step out to "love the Lord your God with all your heart and with all your soul and with all your strength" (Deuteronomy 6:5). How much easier it is to reach out and pick up a newspaper to read than to reach out to pick up the Bible to read! How much easier it is to stay late into the night to watch series of shows on television than to remain, deep into the night, in praise and worship of the reigning monarch, Jesus Christ of Nazareth! How could such a practice be so if there were not a Satan who would do everything in his limited power to keep the believer from going all out for the Lord?

Satan loves to offer deceptive alternatives to worshipping God in all sincerity. These satanic alternatives to wholehearted devotion to God are craftily designed by the Devil to keep us lukewarm, making us, at best, to be of no threat at all to him and his kingdom of darkness. If Satan could steer us away from "being on fire for God," then he could render us powerless. But Satan is liar: he cannot coerce us into submission. We belong to Christ, and to Christ alone we pledge our allegiance; Him we will forever worship with all our heart, with all our soul, and with all our strength. All to Jesus we surrender!

Our posture must be like that of Moses. When Pharaoh made his dubious offer in Exodus 10:24 and said, "Go, worship the Lord. Even your women and children may go with you; only leave your flocks and herds behind," Moses replied appropriately, without compromise, "Our livestock too must go with us; not a hoof is to be left behind" (Exodus 10:26). In Old Testament times, livestock were a pivotal element of Jewish people's worship and religious rites. Anyone who approached God in those days with a sacrificial lamb was bound to receive God's attention. That was why God looked with favour on Abel and his offering. But on Cain and his offering, God did not look with favour (Genesis 4:2–5). In our days, Jesus, the Lamb of

God, offers us better access to God through His blood of the new covenant.

What is it about you that Satan desperately desires that you neglect or keep away from God in order to render your worship unacceptable to God? Moses told Pharaoh that "not a hoof is to be left behind." Our response to Satan's seductive offer should be no less: we will worship God with all that we are and with all that we have; we will leave nothing behind that God desires from us. We will render to God in worship what belongs to Him. We will worship our God without reservation, giving unto Him our all in all. Not a mite will we withhold from Him. Abraham did not withhold Isaac from Him; Hannah did not withhold Samuel from Him; Peter did not withhold his boat from Him. We will not withhold from our God our bodies as living sacrifices holy and pleasing to God. This is our spiritual act of worship without reservation.

Prayer

I surrender all to You, my Lord: my life, my wealth, my gifts and talents, my time, my energy, my status, my dreams and ambitions, my affections, and everything, Lord, that You desire of me. They are all Yours without reservation.

Suggested Scriptures for Further Meditation

Deuteronomy 10:12   Joshua 24:13–15   Psalm 63:6–8

CHAPTER 40

"But deliver us from the evil one"

And lead us not into temptation, but deliver us from
the evil one.

—Matthew 6:13

One prayer offered to God over and over again is the Lord's
Prayer. Originally taught by Jesus to His disciples, the Lord's
Prayer is continuously offered in communion with God during
individual devotional periods in homes, during congregational
worship in churches, upon the outdooring of infants, at
weddings and many other joyous occasions, at mealtimes
in many homes, at the start of the day's work in offices and
workplaces, and also at the gravesite, when a person's task
on earth is done and the time to say goodbye to the departed
soul arrives. The Son of God, who once lived physically on
this planet and experienced also the troubles of this life, first
offered this prayer to *our Father, who art in heaven.*

In this prayer, the Lord Jesus addresses the core issues
that relate to our relationship with God and also the core issues
that pertain to our daily livelihood on earth: our spiritual and

physical well-being. Not only do we need the forgiveness of our sins, but we also need our daily bread, whether we are rich or poor, great or small. Whenever I watch CNN's coverage of the scenes on the floor of the New York Stock Exchange, I see men and women pace back and forth, sometimes with two or more telephone receivers clinging to their earlobes, looking for stocks to trade in. When I watch CNN's documentary *World's Untold Stories,* I sometimes see pictures of hungry children in certain cities scavenging through mountains of refuse, looking for food to eat. In both scenarios, whether on the stock exchange floor or on the refuse dump, one thing is constant: people are looking for their daily bread. "Give us this day our daily bread," said Jesus in the Lord's Prayer.

With the heightened insecurity of our world today, caused not only by divorces, tsunamis, and terrorists' bombs, but also by financial crisis almost everywhere, in both developed and developing countries, Jesus' request to the Father, "And lead us not into temptation, but deliver us from the evil one," is evermore real, really real. Jesus knows about the Evil One, whom He once called the Father of Lies (John 8:44), who comes only to steal and kill and destroy (John 10:10).

More than ever before, and as our focus in this chapter pinpoints, we want to make supplications with strong crying and tears to God (Hebrews 5:7) to *deliver us from the Evil One* and his cohorts (demons and human agents) who are marauding lives in nations and communities, in families, and in offices and workplaces. In one of His longest recorded prayers on behalf of His disciples, Jesus, in John 17:15, prayed to the Father, "Not that you take them out of the world but that you protect them from the evil one." The evil in Satan has not left;

he still prowls around like a roaring lion, looking for someone to devour (1 Peter 5:8).

We need to be humble enough to request prayer support from one another. When the pangs of death by way of the cross grew stronger, Jesus Christ, the Son of God, was humble enough to ask His disciples to stand with Him in prayer (Matthew 26:40). The apostle Paul, in most of his epistles, requested prayer support from his fellow workers and from the churches. In 2 Thessalonians 3:1–3, Paul's request for prayer was "that we may be delivered from wicked and evil men." Then he prayed for God *to strengthen and protect the Thessalonian believers from the Evil One.* During the celebration of the Last Supper with His disciples (Luke 22:31–32), Jesus dropped a bombshell, one that I believe made Peter's chin drop. It was that Satan had incessantly sought to sift (harass) Peter like wheat! "But I have prayed for you," said Jesus, "that your faith may not fail." O that the Lord continuously intercede for us so that we may be delivered from the wicked plans of the Evil One and from the pernicious plans of all those who align themselves with Satan!

One of the greatest blessings we have is God's power of conversion. Whilst we remain in an evil-infested world, God's deliverance also takes the form of conversion. As Joseph said in Genesis 50:20, "But as for you, ye thought evil against me; but God meant it unto good, to bring to pass, as it is this day, to save much people alive." May every evil plan and scheme against you receive the converting intervention of God, bringing to pass God's plans for posterity and the blessing of many others.

Prayer

And lead me not into temptation, *but deliver me from the Evil One.* For Thine is the kingdom and the power and the glory forever. Amen.

Suggested Scriptures for Further Meditation

Psalm 118:10–12   Jeremiah 1:19   Nahum 1:7–8

CHAPTER 41

A GOOD WORK HAS BEGUN

> I thank my God every time I remember you. In all my
> prayers for all of you, I always pray with joy because
> of your partnership in the gospel from the first day
> until now, being confident of this, that He who began
> a good work in you will carry it on to completion until
> the day of Christ .Jesus.
>
> —Philippians 1:3–6

Getting ready to start a new thing poses a challenge to many people. But with God, getting ready to start a new thing is not a problem. If God can get our minds set on Him, then we will not miss it when He starts something new in our lives or in our generation. For this and every year, God is at work, either to begin a new thing or to continue with what He has already begun in you and with you, with good intentions. God is more than ready to celebrate you one more time this year, as His workmanship created Christ Jesus for good works. With a mind fully set on God Almighty, whose mindset is to do good work in you at all times, including this year, you are set for an exciting experience of God's benevolence, which never ceases. Your confidence in God coupled with your partnership with Him positions you to soar to new heights of fullness and maturity in Christ Jesus.

The apostle Paul expressed his confidence in what God was doing in the lives of the believers in Philippi. You can share in the confidence of the apostle Paul by saying to yourself, "God who has begun a good work in me will carry it on to completion." You've got to personalize that piece of Scripture and say it again and again and again: "God who has begun a good work in me will carry it on to completion until the day of Christ Jesus." What God began to work out in you, His divine plan and purpose for your life, which existed even before you were conceived in your mother's womb, is still on course. God has not abandoned that plan. God is a master craftsman; He is patient and will not take His hands off you until He has achieved His purpose. In the midst of the years, with all the challenges, including the disappointments, plus all the scheming of enemies, God never abandons His interest in us unless we choose to persistently ignore Him.

We need the apostolic and Pauline confidence right at the start of every year and every venture to stir us up to step out with boldness, making faith-filled declarations with our mouths about our prospects in the now and in the future. Come with me into the Word and read a few of these faith-filled declarations. In Psalm 118:6–7, the psalmist declares, "The Lord is with me; I will not be afraid. What can man do to me? The Lord is with me; He is my helper. I will look in triumph on my enemies." In Psalm 138:8, the psalmist continues: "The Lord will fulfill His purpose for me; your love, O Lord, endures forever—do not abandon the works of your hands." You are the work of God's hands; He will not abandon you. In this moment of time, God, who has begun a good work in you, will unveil further aspects of His purpose for you. There are some things God will trim from your life, like a farmer does when he prunes a fruit-bearing branch so that it will even be more fruitful. God's dealings with us are designed to make us more fruitful and useful. I pray that during this period of our lives, God will apply more of these divine dealings. We will become better, wiser, and brighter. If we will cooperate more with God day by day, then we will appreciate why the wise man of Ecclesiastes penned the following about God's workings in our lives: "He has made everything beautiful in its time" (Ecclesiastes 3:11) and "I know that everything God does will endure forever" (Ecclesiastes 3:14).

Burst forth with faith and boast about your God. Look straight into the eyes of every challenge and say, "God is at work in me, and His plans for my life are on course; every day of this year, something good is going to happen to me, for the God of all goodness has His eyes upon me and His ears open unto my cry." By faith, take by the horns the challenges you are facing right now and speak into days ahead like a blood-bought child of God, declaring, "I will not die but live, and proclaim what the Lord has done" (Psalm 118:17). Turn to 2 Samuel 22:29–30 and speak like David to tell God, "You are my lamp, O Lord; the Lord turns my darkness into light. With your help I can *advance* against a troop; with my God I can scale a wall" (emphasis mine).

I italicized the word *advance* in David's proclamation. The word means "to go forward, move forward, move ahead, press forward, move on, proceed, press on, progress, go ahead."

David said that with God's help, no army could stop him from reaching his God-given destiny. Now personalize the words of David and speak to the armies of hell, telling them that God is on your side and that, in this year, they cannot stop you from moving ahead. You will advance, no matter what! Advance; don't retreat. Press forward. You originate from God, and God does not retreat; He moves forward. That is why God asked Moses, when Israel reached the Red Sea, "Why are you crying out to me? Tell the Israelites to move on" (Exodus 14:15). As they moved on, the Red Sea gave way for them to pass through as on dry ground. This year and any other year shall not be a barrier; it will be a platform to advance. Advance, brother; move on, sister; for the Lord God has begun a good work in your life.

The hard times of this year and any other upcoming year will be no match for the power of God, which is at work in you. If hard times show up, then turn to God and His promises. One such promise of God is recorded in Zechariah 12:3; it concerns Jerusalem. But you can personalize this promise by substituting your name for the word *Jerusalem.* The passage reads, "On that day, when all the nations of the earth are gathered against her, I will make Jerusalem an immovable rock for all the nations. All who try to move it will injure themselves." God will make you an immovable rock! In this year and the years to come, anyone who tries to dislocate you from where God has planted you will end up being dislocated and given severe injuries by the power of God. Fear not! God who has begun a good work in you will carry it on to completion. Amen!

Prayer

O Lord my God, my faith has found rest in Your promise that You will bring to a perfect end Your good purposes for my life. In this, I am confident that You will establish me with good success.

Suggested Scriptures for Further Meditation

Genesis 28:20–21   John 6:29   2 Timothy 1:12

CHAPTER 42

THE VOICE OF THE LORD

The voice of the Lord is over the waters; the God of glory thunders, the Lord thunders over the mighty waters. The voice of the Lord is powerful; the voice of the Lord is majestic.

—Psalm 29:3–4

The world we live in is full of voices: our own voices, the voices of people around us, and voices far from us. Advances in communications technology have made it possible to hear voices across the globe and even voices of astronauts from the International Space Station. Some voices carry the weight of power and authority; they cannot be ignored. Other voices are mere noises; no one cares about what they say. Most of the voices we hear are those of humans like ourselves. But there are voices that are not of human origin: these are voices attributable to deities. In the book of Revelation, in the messages to the seven churches, it is written severally, "He who has an ear, let him hear what the Spirit says to the churches." God speaks; Jesus speaks; the Holy Spirit speaks. The voice of the Trinity is loud and clear.

At the start of creation, God's voice was heard saying, "Let there be light." Since then and throughout all generations, including our generation, God has been speaking. Adam and Eve were said to have "heard the voice of the Lord God walking in the garden in the cool of the day: and Adam and his wife hid themselves from the presence of the Lord" (Genesis 3:8). Unlike Adam and Eve, we shall not hide ourselves when we hear the voice of God. But we shall be like the prophet Isaiah, who, once he heard the voice of God saying, "Who shall I send and who will go?", responded by saying, "Here I am, send me" (Isaiah 6:8). We serve the God whose name is El Shaddai and whose voice runs through all generations. This year will not be an exception, so brace yourself to hear God's voice. When He speaks, things are commanded into being. He is speaking forth things into your life so that it shall be well with you. We remember the Lord Jesus speaking with a loud voice when saying, "Lazarus, come forth!" And he who was dead and had been buried for four days came forth (John 11:1–44). When death heard the authoritative voice of Jesus demanding the release of Lazarus's spirit, death obeyed and let go of Lazarus. Come on, somebody! Say it loud: "I am coming forth; my business is coming forth; my dreams are coming forth; my marriage is coming forth; my promotion is coming forth; my finances are coming forth; my health is coming forth!" If your state of affairs hears the voice of Almighty God, then it will submit to His bidding. In Ezekiel 37, when the dry bones in the valley heard the voice of God through the prophet Ezekiel, they came alive. The Bible says that demons tremble at the sound of His name. If we will by faith declare the name of Jesus over circumstances, then we shall find that circumstances surrender to our demand.

The voice of our God gives direction. Isaiah 30:21 says, "Whether you turn to the right or to the left, your ears will hear a voice behind you, saying, 'This is the way; walk in it.'" This is the promise of God, that He will guide us with His mighty voice so that we stay on the right path of life and not go astray. Jesus said, "My sheep know my voice" (John 10:3). It pays to endeavour to hear the voice of God more than ever before with each passing day. The voice of God is powerful. The psalmist wants us to know that God's voice has an impact on people, things, situations, and circumstances. Let us consider what the psalmist says in Psalm 29:3: "The voice of God is over the waters; ... His voice thunders over mighty waters." Some waters are rough, stormy, and bitter; it takes the voice of God to deal decisively with them and to bring them to order. We can recall the storm that arose on the Sea of Galilee when Jesus and His disciples were travelling across. It took the voice of Jesus to bring that storm under control (Matthew 8:24–27). The waters of Marah were too bitter for Moses and the people of Israel to drink, but, after calling on God, Moses heard the voice of God directing him to the answer to the problem (Exodus 15:23–24). May the voice of God bring to order any rough, stormy, and bitter waters in your life.

The cedar of Lebanon grows very tall and has a very tough, hard stem. The wood from this tree was therefore used to construct commercial and military ships in ancient times. Its tallness and majestic appearance is metaphorically linked to pride and arrogance. The psalmist says the voice of God breaks in pieces the cedars of Lebanon. May God break into pieces every hardened and tough situation in your life. May the voice of God break and bring down the proud and arrogant who sneer at you and look down on you.

The voice of God flashes like lightning; it is electrifying. God's voice has a high voltage. No one in his or her right mind would want to touch with bare hands a cable carrying high-voltage electricity. In Psalm 18, David recounts God's uncompromising response to his cry to Him for deliverance from death. In verse 14, David said this about God: "He sent out His arrows and scattered the foe; lightning in abundance, and He vanquished them." The supernatural voice of God will send *high-voltage* energy on your behalf to make a way for you out of any deep trouble. On the day of Pentecost, divided tongues, like flames of fire, appeared to the 120 disciples and rested on each one of them (Acts 2:3). The disciples, as a result, received power. Your season of receiving and walking in the power of the Holy Spirit is now. God's voice was in that fire, just as His voice spoke out of the burning bush that appeared to Moses on Mount Horeb. The voice of the Lord shakes the desert. The people of Israel spent almost thirty-eight years wandering in the desert of Qadesh-Barnea, far away from the land flowing with milk and honey that was their final destination. Do you feel like you are wandering in a situation, not knowing what to do? Qadesh-Barnea represents a stronghold of undue delay and procrastination. May the voice of God shake the deserts to bring out anyone who is wandering and moving in circles. Wandering leads to loss of opportunities for success and fruitfulness. Our deserts shall be shaken by the voice of the Lord. They will be transformed into a paradise full of springs of water (Isaiah 35:1–2).

The voice of God twists the oaks and strips the forests bare. The word *twist* connotes rotation or turning. The earth rotates on its axis to bring about day and night. Certain doors to high-street offices turn on their axes to either close or open. Hallelujah! May God twist, rotate, or turn events around for your advantage. May God twist any thing, person, or demon standing tall in opposition against your life. The psalmist goes to say that God's voice strips the forests bare. In the physical realm, certain forests provide hideouts for the wicked to commit heinous crimes such as murder; when the forest is stripped of its dense vegetation, hideouts of the wicked are exposed and the wicked are unable to operate. May God's voice strip any spiritual forest bare wherein demonic forces of wickedness operate to destroy homes, marriages, careers, businesses, and finances.

For the reasons above about what the voice of God does, the psalmist says that when we come into the temple of God, we should shout, "Glory." Somebody shout it: "Glory!"

Prayer

Lord God Almighty, I hear Your welcome voice that calls me nigh to Thee. Like Samuel, I respond by saying, "Lord, speak, for thy servant heareth." Guide my hearing away from the voices that lead people astray. May the power of Your voice work out deliverance for me and my loved ones.

Suggested Scriptures for Further Meditation

Isaiah 40:3   John 3:22   Hebrews 3:7–8

CHAPTER 43

GETTING RID OF THE PREFIX *DIS*

And Joshua said, Hereby ye shall know that the
living God is among you, and that he will without fail
drive out from before you the Canaanites, and the
Hittites, and the Hivites, and the Perizzites, and the
Girgashites, and the Amorites, and the Jebusites.

—Joshua 3:10

The journey of the people of Israel from Egypt, where they lived
in bondage, to the Promised Land, where they lived in freedom
and prosperity, was characterized by many challenging events.
No sooner had they left Egypt than they were pursued from
behind by the elite army of Pharaoh with the aim to capture
and return them to bondage. By divine intervention, the army
of Pharaoh was overthrown in the Red Sea and the Israelites
progressed into the wilderness and journeyed towards the
Promised Land. We bring into remembrance these mighty acts
of God. By faith, I reiterate that anyone pursuing you with the
intention of drawing you away from reaching your goal will be
overthrown by the outstretched arm of God.

After wandering in the wilderness for forty years, the people of Israel finally reached the edge of Jordan. Beyond this lay the Promised Land. The River Jordan in those days was a mighty flowing river which, at certain seasons, overflowed its banks, bringing massive flooding to the outlying plains. It was during one such overflow of the Jordan that Joshua and the people of Israel arrived there. But once again, through divine intervention, the Jordan River was cut off, enabling God's people to walk across the riverbed and onto dry ground. The "Jordan River" of your times will give way to you as you march on to the realization of our dreams. Divine assistance is on your side; press on to your place of abundance in this life.

Beyond the Jordan, however, there were enemies in front of the Jews who had occupied grounds and lands that God had promised to Israel by an oath. One more time, God came to intervene, bringing words of assurance that He would certainly drive out before the Israelites the Canaanites, Hittites, Hivites, Perizittes, Girgashites, Amorites, and Jebusites. I don't know whether you can see what is common about these people who were occupying Israel's inheritance. Their names all end with the four-letter suffix –*ites.* In our times, these "Ites" represent enemies who oppose our entry into our place of honour and promotion, and our access to financial, physical, social, emotional, and spiritual well-being. They are tough, stubborn, and Satan-resourced. But they are subject to defeat, defeat by whoever is Spirit-led and whoever leans on God's Word and believes in the power of Jesus' name.

In Joshua's time, God drove out from the land all the "Ites"; in our time, our changeless and matchless God still drives "Ites" out. In our times, however, the "Ites" have changed their names without changing their character, mission, and modus operandi. They now are described by words prefixed by *dis–*. Have you observed that a number of English words beginning with the prefix *dis* imply terror and torment on humanity? Take an angry look at the following words: *disease, discomfort, discouragement, disappointment, disturbance, dismay, distress, disorder, disgrace, disillusion, disheartening, dismissal, disenchantment, dismal, disaster, dissatisfaction, disobedience,* and so on. For many people, these words and what they stand for or mean are the things that have kept them away from possessing their God-purposed inheritance in this life.

Joshua and his people were faced with the "Ites" many years before Christ was born. We are faced with the "dis" many years after Christ was crucified. But I am comforted by the fact that the God who drove away before Joshua the "Ites" is the same God who is with us and who has promised, "Never will I leave you; never will I forsake you" (Hebrews 13:5). So whether faced by "Ites" or by "dis," we are marching on to victory, to possess the best God has purposed for our lives on this planet.

If *dis*ease should rise up against us, then we will anchor on the provision God has made through Christ, by whose stripes we are healed (Isaiah 53:5). In times of *dis*comfort, we will call on the God of all comfort who comforts us so that we can comfort those in any trouble with the comfort we ourselves have received from God (2 Corinthians 1:3–4). We will not be *dis*couraged; for the Lord God, our God, is with us; He will neither fail us nor forsake us" (1 Chronicles 28:20). *Dis*appointment shall not be our portion, for it is written, "The hope of the righteous shall not be cut off" (Proverbs 23:18).

We will resist any attempt by the Devil to bring *dis*order to our homes, workplaces, and schools, for our God is not a God of disorder (1 Corinthians 14:33). *Dis*aster shall not overtake us, for we will take refuge in the shadow of God's wings until the disaster has passed (Psalm 57:1b). *Dis*grace shall not come near our gates, for in Isaiah 54:4, God says that we should not be afraid; we shall not suffer shame; we should not fear disgrace; we will not be humiliated. We will obey and not *dis*obey the Lord, for we know that to obey is better than sacrifice, and to heed is better than the fat of rams (1 Samuel 15:22b).

How did Joshua and Israel overcome and triumph over the Canaanites, Hittites, Hivites, Perizittes, Girgashites, Amorites, and Jebusites? Joshua, who was the leader of Israel at that time, surrendered to the commander of the army of the Lord (Joshua 5:13–14). Our victory over the entire "dis" group of tormentors rests with our daily submission to the Lord Jesus. In his surrender to the commander, Joshua received instructions about the strategy for each of the battles he fought against the "Ites," one after the other. As a result, Joshua conquered thirty-one kings by the time of his old age. He is credited with leading his people to dispossess the "Ites" and to possess their inheritance. Let's raise a war cry; we are getting rid of every "dis" in our lives. Whatever "dis" is threatening your life shall fall. You will walk over it in triumph, as Joshua did when he brought down the walls of Jericho and subdued the kings of all the "Ites." March on to victory in Jesus' name! You are more than a conqueror through Christ Jesus, who strengthens you.

Prayer

Lord Jesus Christ, You are the Holy One who goes ahead of me on this life's journey to possess my inheritance that I have in You. You already assured me of victory when You said, "Be of good cheer for I have overcome the world." In Your name, therefore, I prevail over every dis on my way and in my life.

Suggested Scriptures for Further Meditation

Isaiah 41:10   Isaiah 54:4   Psalm 103:3

CHAPTER 44

BEING AWARE OF THE GIBEONITES

The Israelites sampled their provisions but did not inquire of the Lord. ... Three days after they made the treaty with the Gibeonites, the Israelites heard that they were neighbors, living near them.

—Joshua 9:14,16

O the Gibeonites! How I can't bear them! They are the equivalent of our modern-day "419" gangsters. The term *419* was coined in Nigeria to describe fraudsters. With Satan at the helm of affairs, deception and all forms of craftiness intended to outwit the undiscerning continue to claim more victims. Like Joshua and the elders of Israel, we only get to know of the scam after we have fallen victim. God forbid in our days that Gibeonites swindle us! So we've got to hoist our antennae of discernment high into the realms of the Spirit and, with the help of the Holy Spirit, pick out and decode the cunning signals and dubious movements of Satan, his host of lying demons, and his human collaborators.

What on earth happened to Joshua, a man who had all the resources and privileges from God on his side that he was able to be outwitted by conmen? How important it is for us to be in constant communication with God! In Joshua 9, Joshua had gone to Ai a second time and had conquered it. He was marching on to take the next territory. Having heard and seen what Joshua had done to Jericho and Ai, the rest of the kings gathered themselves together to fight against Joshua and Israel. Watch out! Enemies are gathering for battle because of the progress you've made in life. But they will surely fail; they will stumble and fall at your feet.

But watch out; again I say, watch out. Some enemies like to fight against you headlong, in an attempt to overpower you. Others, like the Gibeonites, use other means to get a way into your life and stay without your conquering them. They seek a form of cohabitation, but one tainted with deception. The Bible says that when the Gibeonites heard what Joshua had done to Jericho and Ai, they resorted to a ruse; in other words, they acted *craftily* (Joshua 9:3). Let me say it again: some enemies will not fight you because they know you are more powerful than they, and so they will resort to a ruse. *Ruse* means "trick, dodge, wile, con, scam, hoax, deception, ploy, or stunt." Let us not forget that we have an arch-enemy, Satan, who is exceptionally crafty and deceitful. Better watch out! The Gibeonites got old clothes and bags and secured stale bread to make themselves appear as if they had been on a long journey. After doing this, they came to Joshua's camp and asked him to make a covenant with them.

With whom do you strike partnership in marriage, business, and ministry? In Deuteronomy 20:10–18, God told the

Israelites how to deal with the people occupying their land. These Gibeonites were living within the land but didn't want the Israelites to know it. So they presented themselves to Joshua as servants. When Joshua asked them who they were, they told a subtle lie, which Joshua, unfortunately, believed. Have you believed in a lie? Joshua and the other leaders of Israel acted according to their own understanding rather than obeying God. They were deceived and taken in by what their eyes saw.

We can become so preoccupied and busy with the work we are doing that we neglect God, who sustains, directs, and protects us. When we are busy, we sometimes fail to connect to God. Even if God calls to warn us, we have our spiritual or intuitive phones off or else we are outside the coverage area. We cannot be reached by God. We must stay in constant communication with God. We do this by being in the Word, in prayer, and in worship. We need to talk with God and seek His wisdom. He will give us insight into any situation. Joshua and the elders did not do this; they did not seek the counsel of God. They looked at the testimony of the Gibeonites and based their decisions on what they saw. We don't go by what we see alone, because we can't see everything. Our natural eyes cannot see and interpret everything. We don't know the beginning and the end of many things of life. We need a God who knows the beginning from the end and the end from the beginning. We need a God who knows the inside out of every matter. We have to go by what the Word of God says and not lean on our own understanding, as Proverbs 3:5–6 tells us: "Trust the Lord with all your heart and lean not on your own understanding; in all your ways acknowledge Him and He will make your paths straight."

Joshua and the elders knew the Word, but they ignored it and allowed themselves to be governed by what they saw rather than consulting God. Eve listened to a lie of the Serpent, even though she knew the Word of God. She did not stop in the middle of her conversation with the Serpent to ask God what to do. Have our easy-going, fast-lane, digitalized, twenty-first-century lives made us forget God and become lax in our communication with Him? Some believers would rather spend hours on end watching cat-and-mouse cartoon series than bending a knee to pray that God bind demons who lie. No wonder when the Gibeonites surface in our marriages, homes, and businesses they take away from us and share in our inheritance.

In this twenty-first century, we cannot afford to leave communicating with God out of the equation. Note that the Internet has made the Gibeonites of our generation even more subtle. Three days after making the covenant with the Gibeonites, the Israelites learned that the Gibeonites were next door, that Israel had been lied to and deceived. We have all, at one point in time or another, been deceived. But not again, not this time!

Prayer

I acknowledge You, O Lord God, and trust Your promise to guide and guard me in all my ways. In a world made more insecure by the satanic order of fraud, lies, and deception, I turn my ears and eyes of discernment to You so that You may share with and reveal to me the truth, nothing but the truth, about matters of life that I encounter, lest I become a victim of modern-day Gibeonites.

Suggested Scriptures for Further Meditation

John 8:44   2 Corinthians 11:3   1 Thessalonians 3:5

CHAPTER 45

O THE BLOOD OF JESUS!

> For you know that it was not with perishable things
> such as silver or gold that you were redeemed from
> the empty way of life handed down to you from your
> ancestors, but with the precious blood of Christ, a
> lamb without blemish or defect.
>
> —1 Peter 1:18–19

O the blood that Jesus shed for us way back on Calvary! This is the blood that gives us strength from day to day! It will never, ever lose its power! What can make us whole again? Nothing but the blood of Jesus! How precious is the flow that makes us white as snow! There is no fountain we know of that cleanses us inside out as does the blood of Jesus. (The opening statements of this chapter are excerpts from Bible-based hymns and choruses popular among believers in the kingdom of God.) There is no dispute: there can be no redemption without the blood of Jesus.

Christ Jesus, the Bible says, is the Lamb of God who was slain before the foundation of this world was laid. In other words, God made provision for the Lamb's blood to be the basis for any meaningful and lasting fellowship between Himself and humankind. When Adam and Eve fell from Eden and lost fellowship with God, God, in His mercy, provided animal skins for them to cover their nakedness, or sinfulness (Genesis 3:21). Obviously, an animal had to be slain and its blood shed in order for its skin to be used to cover sin in Eden.

Genesis 4:4–5 tells us that God had respect and regard for Abel's offering, but for Cain and his offering, God had no respect or regard. The secret of Abel's superior and acceptable offering was the fact that it involved the shedding of the blood of a sheep on the altar. Abel, as it were, approached God through the blood of a lamb, as if he could read in God's mind that the way to God was through the Lamb, Jesus Christ (Hebrews 11:4).

Many, many years later after Abel's replica lamb was offered, the real Lamb of God who takes away the sins of the world proclaimed to the hearing of His disciples, "I am the Way and the Truth and the Life; no one comes to the Father but by me" (John 14:6). As the Lamb of God, Jesus shed His blood to atone for our sins in order to make way for a lasting fellowship between us and God. Jesus did not donate His blood; He shed His blood. Good Friday was the bloodiest day in human history. One Man, Jesus, shed a great deal of blood from His head, hands, feet, back, and side in order to atone for the sins of the entire human race.

O the blood of Jesus! By it, Jesus loosed us and freed us from our sins (Revelation 1:5). The guilt of sin cannot stand the power of Christ's blood. Once we confess our sins, we obtain God's forgiveness through the blood of Jesus (Colossians 1:14). His blood purifies our bodies and consciences of dead works (Hebrews 9:13–14). The miracles Moses performed by the hand of God in Egypt could not persuade Pharaoh to let go the people of Israel from bondage. But when the Passover lambs were slaughtered and their blood was applied to the lintels above the doors and on the two side posts of the Israelites' houses, God sent a devouring angel to strike the Egyptians' firstborn sons and firstborn livestock in every home without the sign of the blood (Exodus 12:22–23,29). Pharaoh's grip on the people of Israel was broken, and he let the people go. Jesus Christ is the true Passover Lamb. With His blood, He paid our ransom fee and purchased us from our bondage to sin and Satan (Revelation 5:9).

Through His blood we are washed clean, each time we confess any known sin. His blood pleads forgiveness and cleanses us; we are therefore able to appear before God without any sin, filth, or guilt. We will arrive in heaven in robes washed white in the blood of the Lamb (Revelation 7:14). Hallelujah! Through His blood, we maintain our righteousness before God. His blood renders null and void Satan's accusations and charges against us. By His blood, and by our constant testifying of our faith in His finished work for us on Calvary's cross, we overcome the Devil (Revelation 12:11). Satan trembles at the sight of Jesus' blood. That's why believers sing and say, "I am gonna stay right under the blood so the Devil can't do me no harm." In Egypt, the angel of death did not go near any house with the sign of the blood of the Passover lambs.

The blood of Christ speaks; it is blood with an authoritative and intercessory voice. In Hebrews 12:24, we are told that the sprinkled blood of Jesus speaks a better, nobler, and more gracious message than the blood of Abel, which cried out for vengeance when Cain killed him (Genesis 4:10). If we sin and confess it, then the blood of Jesus cries out to God, pleading, "Father, forgive them!" No need to carry on with an unconfessed sin; it is a needless burden to bear. If we confess our sins, then God is faithful and just to forgive our sins. The blood of His Son, Jesus Christ, cleanses us from all guilt and unrighteousness (1 John 1:7–9). The blood that oozed from His stripes provides for our healing (Isaiah 53:4–5). Blood poured out from His head once the crown of thorns was forced upon it. This blood cancelled and overturned every curse. Yes, in the blood we prevail and win every battle. His blood never loses its power.

Prayer

Lord Jesus, I appreciate Your blood, by which You ransomed me from the power of Satan and from the bondage of sin. In Your blood, I prevail. In Your blood, I win my battles. In Your blood, victory is mine.

Suggested Scriptures for Further Meditation

Exodus 12:13   Colossians 1:14   Hebrews 9:22

CHAPTER 46

SERVING THE KING

> David came to Saul and entered his service. Saul
> liked him very much, and David became one of
> his armor-bearers. Then Saul sent word to Jesse,
> saying, "Allow David to remain in my service, for I
> am pleased with him."
>
> —1 Samuel 16:21–22

"Who is on the Lord's side? Who will serve the King?" These
are the opening lines of the first stanza of the hymn penned
in 1877 by Frances Havergal. It was and still is our call to
the service of our God and His kingdom. Some cringe at the
thought of being called to serve God. I don't understand their
fears and hesitation; but O what a privilege to be an instrument
in the hands of God! When God takes hold of your life or,
rather, when you allow God access to your life, putting all your
talents and goods and expertise at His disposal, you become
an invaluable asset to God and a blessing to humankind.

Kings, and I mean wise kings, take pride in the success,
wealth, strength, and well-being of their kingdom. Anyone who
is loyal to the king and seeks the prosperity of the kingdom

and the well-being of the king becomes a bosom-friend of the king. The king takes delight in such a person. When a person pleases a king, he or she is given special care and attention by the king, and the king honours this person exceedingly abundantly. In Bible times, records abound of such honours and rewards given to individuals who rendered delightful service(s) to kings and their kingdoms.

The Scripture quotation that opens this chapter recounts David's initial entrance into the service of King Saul. King Saul had a need. His relationship with God had fallen apart, and he was losing grip of the kingdom. Disturbed by his condition, Saul made a search for a talented musician to play the harp. Whenever David played the harp, the king was delivered from an evil spirit that tormented him. In this way, David brought deliverance and comfort to the king. David was the choice musician; he used his talent to serve the interest and purpose of King Saul. As a result, David the shepherd-boy became David the music-boy at the king's palace. What an honour to play in the king's presence! Later on, when the kingdom of Saul was threatened by Goliath, Saul made an offer of great wealth to any man who would take on Goliath, kill him, and save Israel (1 Samuel 16:25). The rewards also included the giving of the king's daughter in marriage. Once again, David rose to the occasion. He defeated Goliath and won the prize. We know the story well enough to remember that David went on to become the next king of Israel after Saul died.

When King Nebuchadnezzar conquered Jerusalem, he took as captives young, intelligent Israelis from the royal family and nobility, whom he trained for entering into his service in Babylon. In case you don't know, you have been chosen by the

King of Kings and the Lord of Lords to serve in His kingdom (1 Peter 2:9). Later on, King Nebuchadnezzar had a troubling dream that required interpretation. Daniel, through revelation by God, interpreted the dream. Guess what?! The king placed Daniel in a high position and lavished many gifts on him (Daniel 2:46–48).

This reminds me of Joseph, who used his gift for interpreting dreams to resolve a mysterious dream of Pharaoh. Joseph, then incarcerated in prison, was rewarded with the number-two position of political power in Egypt. The slave-boy became a prime minister because he served a king and his kingdom with the talents, or divine gifts, with which God had endowed him. Like Joseph, you are endowed with talents, gifts, and expertise. What are you doing on earth with your talents, gifts, and expertise to serve God and your country?

The first chapter of the book of Esther gives an account of a domestic dispute in the palace of King Xerxes. Vashti, the wife of the king, had acted in a manner that was considered inappropriate to the dignity of his majesty, the king. She was divorced by the king. Thereafter, a search was made for a new queen as a replacement. Esther, an orphan, then a captive in the kingdom of Xerxes, entered into the contest of finding a successor to the ousted queen. By her beauty and with the grace of God upon her, Esther became the next queen (Esther 2:16–17). Later on, she used her position as queen to serve the purpose of God to preserve the Jewish people from the threat posed by Haman, an avowed enemy of the Jews.

No one serves the interest of a king and his kingdom and goes unrewarded. If the kingdoms of this world reward handsomely their faithful and loyal citizens, then can you fathom what reward awaits those who love God and faithfully serve the purposes of God's kingdom? The apostle Paul says in 1 Corinthians 1:9, "What eye has not seen and ear has not heard and has not entered into the heart of man, has God prepared for those who love Him and are called to serve His purpose." What are you doing in the kingdom of Jesus Christ? He is our King and wants to see us at our posts, working to serve Him and His kingdom (John 4:31–36).

> Who is on the Lord's side? Who will serve the King?
> Who will be His helpers, other lives to bring? Who
> will leave the world's side? Who will face the foe?
> Who is on the Lord's side? Who for Him will go? By
> Thy call of mercy, by Thy grace divine; we are on
> the Lord's side—Savior, we are Thine!
>   —Frances R. Havergal, 1877

Prayer

O Lord, my majestic King, I desire to serve You. Help me avail myself to You in accordance with Your plans for my life and in consonance with the talents, skills, and gifts with which You have graciously endowed me.

Suggested Scriptures for Further Meditation

1 Samuel 12:24   Matthew 22:37   Psalm 95:2–3

CHAPTER 47

GOD'S PREVAILING PURPOSE

> Now the Lord was gracious to Sarah as he had said,
> and the Lord did for Sarah what he had promised.
> Sarah became pregnant and bore a son to Abraham
> in his old age, at the very time God had promised
> him.
>
> —Genesis 21:1–2

I am baffled by God's tenacity, God's ability to keep on course His plans and purposes despite satanic plots and machinations against those plans and purposes. God never cuts corners. Neither we nor Satan can push God to the wall to hurry up and do things our way or push God to accept our alternatives to His original plans and purposes. Because of our human frailty coupled with our inability to know everything or to understand the totality of God's dealings with us, including His timing and appointed seasons, we are more often than not tempted to accelerate events. We think God is too slow at times. Since we are in a hurry to get things done, we try to move on without God.

We will, however, do ourselves a lot of good if we heed the words of the Lord God: "'For my thoughts are not your thoughts, neither are your ways My ways,' says the Lord. 'For as the heavens are higher than the earth, so are My ways higher than your ways and my thoughts than your thoughts'" (Isaiah 55:8–9). The fact of the matter is that God's purpose for your life will prevail regardless of tens of thousands of enemies who rise up against you, as long as you listen to God and follow His ways. God does not abandon His purposes even if we turn aside for short-lived substitutes or alternatives. I am very glad that God did not settle for Ishmael, Abraham's son before Isaac and who was born from the womb of Hagar, but kept to His original plan of a son (Isaac) to be born through the womb of Sarah.

Abraham was eighty-six years old when Hagar bore Ishmael; it was the arrangement between Sarah and Abraham for the latter to sleep with Hagar and have a child. Sarah, then barren, could not consider herself ever giving birth to a child, despite God's promise that He would give Abraham a son through her (Genesis 17:16). In fact, Abraham himself laughed at the thought of Sarah's ever giving birth and so told God to forget about the idea of a son by Sarah and to rather accept Ishmael as the right alternative (Genesis 17:17–18). But God refused to be coerced into endorsing Ishmael as heir apparent to Abraham. In Genesis 17:18, God told Abraham that it was through Isaac, not Ishmael, that He was to establish His covenant. O how often we plead with God to forget about His original plan and to accept our substitutes, our own plans!

Thank God that He did not go with Abraham's corner-cutting strategy. I pray that God sticks with His original plans and purposes for our lives, irrespective of our cries and desperation for Him to accept our inpatient, doubt-induced, corner-cutting substitutes. This is my prayer. May God open your eyes to see wisdom and eternal blessings in what He has purposed for you. May you overcome the temptation induced by peer pressure and the deceptions of Satan to rush for that which does not truly satisfy. Wait for God's purpose to mature at its appointed time and you will never regret you waited for it. There can be no substitute for God's original purpose!

If the prodigal son had waited to realize his father's original purpose for him as heir apparent, he would not have taken shortcut measures to access his inheritance prematurely. All the mess the prodigal son went through would have been avoided. But God had mercy on him, for when he came back to his senses, he returned home to his father's love and original plan (Luke 15:17–22). Proverbs 3:5–6 admonishes, "Trust the Lord with all your heart and lean not on your own understanding. In all your ways acknowledge Him and He will direct your paths." Shortcuts and quick fixes are two of the greatest enemies to true success in life. Anyone who thinks God is too slow in carrying out His purposes has got it all wrong. How can God Almighty, who spent six days creating the heavens and the earth and everything they contain, ever be too slow? No, God is never too slow; rather, we are in a hurry to acquire things or to become what God never intends for us.

God's purposes will always prevail. His purposes for Joseph prevailed despite the plots of Joseph's own brothers. His purpose for David prevailed despite David's own weaknesses and the plots of King Saul. His purposes for Peter prevailed despite Peter's impulsiveness and denials of Jesus. His purposes for humankind through the Messiah, the seed of a woman who would save the world, prevailed despite opposition from Satan's kingdom of darkness. There would have been less trouble in Abraham's home if he had not tried to substitute Ishmael for Isaac. Say no to any pressure to abandon God's purpose for your life. Stay with God; you are safe with Him and in Him.

Prayer

I believe in You, Lord. I believe in Your plans for my life. Help me fix my eyes on You as You unfold Your plans according to the times and seasons You have appointed. I resist any pressure inspired by hell that is intended to push me out of Your plans. Help me, Lord.

Suggested Scriptures for Further Meditation

Psalm 33:11   Proverbs 19:21   Isaiah 46:10

CHAPTER 48

ALL IN THE BLOOD

> But you have come to Mount Zion and to the city
> of the living God, the heavenly Jerusalem, and to
> myriads of angels, to the general assembly and
> church of the firstborn who are enrolled in heaven,
> and to God, the Judge of all, and to the spirits of the
> righteous made perfect, and to Jesus, the mediator
> of a new covenant, and to the sprinkled blood, which
> speaks better than the blood of Abel.
>
> —Hebrews 12:22–24

Of all fluids in the animal body (including the human body), blood is the most versatile and the most mysterious. Life, according to the Scriptures, is in the blood (Leviticus 17:11). Blood is sacred. God values blood. In a biology class many years ago, I first learned about blood as the medium of transport for everything essential for the nourishment, sustenance, and maintenance of the body. There is oxygen in the blood; there are enzymes and co-enzymes in the blood; there are vitamins in the blood; there are hormones in the blood; there are antigens and antibodies in the blood; there are minerals and trace metals in the blood. There is life in the blood.

Beyond the physical, blood has a mysterious connection with the soul. For as long as blood flows in the body, the soul can inhabit the body. We cannot understand it all, but certainly God has attached sacredness to blood and particularly to the shedding of blood. Hebrews 9:22 says that under the law, almost everything is purified by means of blood. Without the shedding of blood, there is no remission of sin. The wholeness of the human spirit and soul therefore depends on the application of prescribed blood: the blood of the Mediator between God and humankind. It is and must be the blood of the Lamb, the Lord Jesus Christ. It is the blood with a voice that speaks grace upon humanity, that speaks and pleads mercy over the soul of humankind.

On this very matter, Jesus was emphatic and pointed out to humankind that His blood was the blood approved for cleansing the soul from all sin, making it possible for us to be presented blameless before God. In the words of Jesus, everything we need in order to come into fellowship with God and to remain in fellowship with God is in His blood. All is in His blood. In John 6:53–56, Jesus spoke thus: "I tell you the truth, unless you eat of the flesh of the Son of Man and drink His blood, you have no life in you. Whoever eats my flesh and drinks my blood has eternal life, and I will raise him up at the last day. For my flesh is real food and my blood is real drink. Whoever eats my flesh and drinks my blood remains in me, and I in him." This is hard talk. Jesus said His blood is real drink; everything for the well-being of our spirit, soul, and body is in His blood. It is all in the blood!

What are the things His blood apportions for us? Have you ever thought about them? Maybe you have, but let's move on.

In His blood, we have redemption, the forgiveness of our sins (Ephesians 1:7; Colossians 1:14). Through His blood, we have been brought nigh to share in the covenant promises otherwise exclusively reserved for Abraham and his descendants. Abraham's blessings are therefore ours. There are blessings in Christ's blood. In His blood, we are justified and made right with God (Romans 5:9), as God no longer treats us as sinners. The wrath of God that would have been poured on us has been turned away by the blood of Jesus.

There is power in His blood to break curses. By His death on the cross, Jesus took upon Himself curses incurred by us as a result of our sins and acts of lawlessness (Galatians 3:13). By His blood, Jesus has broken those curses, for He paid in full the price of our iniquities. In the days of Moses in Egypt, it was the blood of the Passover lambs that overcame the curse imposed on firstborns. Christ is our Passover Lamb, and His shed blood breaks the power of curses. No believer living under the covering of the blood of Jesus can be cursed. The snare of curse is broken through His blood.

There is healing in His blood. The stripes inflicted on Jesus' body drew blood. The Bible gives reasons for why so much blood was drawn from His body by those stripes. The blood from the stripes is a fountain of healing for all manner of diseases, as explained in Isaiah 53:4–5. The blood of Jesus still confronts and overpowers sicknesses and diseases. It is by faith in His name that we apply the healing power of His blood over the sick and afflicted. We should not be tired of pleading the blood of Jesus over loved ones and relations afflicted by sicknesses. Whenever we plead the blood of Jesus over people, circumstances, and situations, we are like Moses sprinkling the blood of slain calves and goats over people and articles to render them whole, to make them fit for use, and to seal them for God's covenant blessings.

In our opening quotation for this chapter, the Bible says that as believers we have come to Jesus, the Mediator of a new covenant, and *to the sprinkled blood,* which speaks of better and nobler things than does the blood of Abel. The power of intercession is in the blood of Jesus. The sprinkled blood of Jesus does far more than the blood that Moses sprinkled. You have come to this sprinkled blood. This blood turns upside down anything instigated from hell. Because we have come to the sprinkled blood, we are to invoke the intervention of that blood in every situation that confronts us. I get excited when I hear people pray and say, "I plead the blood of Jesus."

Prayer

Thank You, Jesus, for Your blood, which ratified the new covenant. By Your blood, we overcome the ancient Serpent, the Devil. Also through Your blood we are able to render null and void any accusations levelled against us from the pit of hell. Your blood has made us whole and vindicated us. We appropriate the healing contained in Your blood. By prayer, we amplify the voice of Your precious blood against the gates of hell. We clinch victory today and every day through Your blood.

Suggested Scriptures for Further Meditation

John 3:24–25   Ephesians 2:13   Colossians 1:20

CHAPTER 49

THE GOD OF SET TIME

But when the time had fully come, God sent his Son, born of a woman, born under law, to redeem those under law, that we might receive the full rights of sons.

—Galatians 4:4–5

In this life we live on earth, it is not uncommon to hear the expressions, "We are running out of time," "We are getting late," "We've got to meet the deadline," "It's about time I made a move," "What is the best time?", etc. The opening chapter of the book of Acts records a discourse between the risen Lord Jesus and His disciples on the matter of time. The disciples asked the Lord, "Is this the time when you will re-establish the kingdom and restore it to Israel" (Acts 1:6)? I wonder what questions about time may be running through your mind.

For many aspects of our lives, it is not too difficult to know at what time to do what thing. The average civil or public servant knows when to leave home for office and when to close from work. The student knows when to be in class for the next lecture. But there are other matters of this life for which it is not as easy to know when it is right or appropriate to do something, to have something, or to make a move. King Solomon, the author of the book of Ecclesiastes, says in verse 3:1 that "to everything there is a season, and a time for every matter or purpose under heaven." That's good news; but how do we discern the appropriate times and seasons? It was said of the sons of Issachar that they understood the times and therefore knew what Israel ought to do (1 Chronicles 12:32).

I find consolation in God our Father and Jesus Christ our Saviour for their perfect timing. God has not abandoned us on earth without guidance, indicators, or promptings as to the right time or season to have something, to do something, or to make a move. When the time was ripe for Jacob to leave the home of his treacherous uncle (Laban), God spoke to him and said, "Return to the land of your fathers and to your people and I will be with you" (Genesis 31:3). When the wine ran out during the wedding reception in Cana and Jesus' mother came to Him to inform Him of the lack of wine, He answered His mother with the words, "My time to act has not come" (John 2:4). At another occasion, when Jesus' brothers tried to push Him to go to a Jewish festival and show Himself there, His response to them was, "My time has not come yet" (John 7:6). If we follow Him who knows the times and seasons to do what is right in conformance to the purposes of God and for God's pleasure, then we can trust Him to prompt us when it is just right to do something, to have something, or to make a move in the matters that are critical to God's will for our lives. In Ecclesiastes 8:5–6, it is written, "A wise man's mind will know both when and what to do. For every purpose and matter has its (right) time and judgment" (AMP).

Will God, who says He knows the plans He has for you, deny you knowledge of the timeliness of those plans? No, because God desires that you step in line and in time with Him. In our opening Bible quotation for this chapter, the apostle Paul uses the phrase "when the time had fully come." When the fullness of time had come, in other words, at the proper time, God sent His Son, born of a woman, to purchase freedom for us. Jesus stepped into human history at the right time: at God's set time. He came at the right time to create an enabling environment for our salvation. When, then, is the best time for a person's salvation? The answer is, "Today." For it is written, "Therefore, as the Holy Spirit says: Today, if you will hear His voice, do not harden your hearts" (Hebrews 3:7–8). In 2 Corinthians 6:2, the Word of God declares, "In the time of favour I have listened to and heeded your call. ... Now is the acceptable time; now is the day of salvation."

One day, Jesus, upon approaching Jerusalem, wept over the city (Luke 19:41–44). Jesus prophesied that trouble would brew over Jerusalem because the people of the city, notably the Pharisees, scribes, and religious leaders, did not recognize their day of visitation. What a tragedy it is when God visits His people and many of them miss His visitation! God does not want you to miss your "day of visitation." A day of visitation is God's set time for your breakthrough: deliverance from trouble; healing; promotion; connection with a would-be life partner; a new job; etc. How often people miss their appointed time with God because they stayed away from church or a prayer meeting on a particular day—or they simply refused to listen to the leading of the Holy Spirit!

Listen to the prayer of Abraham's servant Eliezer as he stood by a well, believing in God for a wife for Isaac:

> O Lord, God of my master Abraham, I pray You, cause me to meet with good success today, and show kindness to my master Abraham. See, I stand here by the well of water and the daughters of the men of the city are coming to draw water. And let it be that the girl to whom I say, I pray you, let down your jar that I may drink, and she replies Drink and I will give your camels drink also—let her be the one whom you have selected and appointed and indicated to your servant Isaac to be a wife to him. ... Before he had finished speaking, behold, out came Rebecca. (Genesis 24:12–15)

It was the day of God's appointment for Isaac and Rebecca to come out of being single and move into being married. The servant got to the well at the right time. So did Rebecca, who also did the right thing at that appointed time.

We will wait for God's appointed time. May God help us as He did for Abraham! One day whilst at home with his wife, Sarah, Abraham saw three men approaching his tent. He ran to meet them and requested that they not bypass his tent. Abraham and Sarah were, at that time, believing God for a child. Abraham urged the men to stay in his house. He served them water and, later, a delicious meal. It was a day of God's visitation upon this old childless couple; for when the men had finished eating, they pronounced a prophetic word over Abraham and Sarah, saying, "Is anything too hard for God? I

197

will return to you at the appointed time next year, and Sarah will have a son" (Genesis 18:9–14). It happened just as God said, for at the appointed time the following year, Sarah brought forth Isaac (Genesis 21:1–2). Glory be to God!

Your being alive is not an accident. God's clock is ticking towards an appointed time for you and your prayers; your obedience and faith in God is preparing and hastening you towards that day and season. When? I don't know, but you must still wait for the appointed season, for it will surely come. For the God that you serve is the God of set time and seasons. Elisha did not miss his appointed time; he was told that if he saw his master, Elijah, being taken up to heaven, he would inherit the double anointing he was waiting for. God will give you a sign when your time is due. You will take a step at the right time. This is what happened to good old Simeon, as recorded in Luke 2:25–30. Prompted by the Holy Spirit, he went into the temple in Jerusalem on the right day and at the right time to meet and see the baby Jesus, as determined by God. Simeon had been waiting for years to see the birth of the Messiah. He did not die until he saw the salvation of the Lord.

Fear not; God is faithful, and your times are in His hand. In Psalm 102:13, the psalmist cried out in prayer, saying, "You will arise and have compassion on Zion, for it is time to show favour to her; the appointed time has come" (emphasis mine). Is this your prayer, too? The answer must be yes.

Prayer

My Lord and my God, I cannot but thank You for the times past when You carried out Your best intentions in my life. I glorify

You for the times and the seasons which You have appointed in the future to show Your good pleasure towards me. Grant me the grace to discern Your best moments and the faith to take opportunities and reach out for my entitlements in this life as purposed by You.

Suggested Scriptures for Further Meditation

1 Chronicles 12:32　Daniel 2:21　1 Thessalonians 5:1

CHAPTER 50

IN *ALL* THINGS

And we know that in all things God works for the good of those who love him, who have been called according to his purpose.

—Romans 8:2

Give thanks in all circumstances; for this is God's will for you in Christ Jesus.

—1 Thessalonians 5:18

A great preacher, Charles Spurgeon, once said "Defend the Bible? I would as soon defend a lion!" This man believed that every word of God is true and can stand the test of time. The author of Psalm 119 devoted the whole of the psalm to extol the luminosity, reliability, validity, profitability, and probity of God's Word in all issues of life. In the 89th verse of Psalm 119, the author sought to ascribe immortality to God's Word by saying that, "Your word, O Lord, is eternal; it stands firm in the heavens." In the 165th verse, the author extols the dependability of God's Word when he says, "Great peace have they who love your law, and nothing can make them stumble." Amen!

In the face of all these truths in the Bible, how come we sometimes stumble and lose our peace? I am inclined to answer by saying that we stumble and lose our peace of mind because we are unable to come to terms with some exhortations from the Word of God in the face of what we see, hear, and feel, including the excruciating, bone-deep emotional and physical pain, which the storms of life inflict upon us. Seemingly "unreasonable" to our natural mind and our frail humanity are such passages in the Bible as Romans 8:28, which reads, "And we know that *in all things* God works for the good of those who love Him, who have been called according to His purpose," and as 1 Thessalonians 5:18, which reads, "Give thanks *in all circumstances,* for this is God's will for you in Christ Jesus." In all things and in all circumstances! How can God work for good when a loved one passes away? How can one thank God when one's business goes bankrupt?

When all is fair, bright, and rosy, and life flows with milk and honey, the above Spirit-sanctioned exhortations are readily recited by many a Christian. We hail these passages as appropriate and God-sent. But did God breathe these exhortations for "good times" only, or did God intend them to be also applicable in "bad times"? When it is all dark and cloudy and we are unable to see the sunshine of success and good health over our heads, how many of us, sincerely from the heart, are able to remain loyal to God, uphold our confidence in God, and, with a grateful spirit, look straight ahead with an enduring attitude that says, "Even though it is all dark and gloomy, my God is at work and will turn it all for my good" (Habakkuk 3:17–18)? Raise your hand if your answer to the question is yes.

In Romans 8:28, the apostle Paul begins the exhortation with the phrase, "And *we know.*" Paul believed from experience that if any man or a woman, boy or girl, loves God and is walking in the purposes of God for his or her life, no matter what dark, cruel, crushing circumstances come his or her way, then God, who is always gracious and merciful, works to bring out ultimate goodness and to take that person to a profitable end. In all things good or bad, God works for the ultimate good of those who are yielded to Him. Therefore, we are able to thank Him, knowing that His will for our lives, for which reason Christ died on the cross, cannot be altered to our disadvantage by any circumstances. In 2 Timothy 1:12, describing a time when Paul was going through one of his suffocating sufferings, Paul, through the eyes of faith, declared, "*I know* whom I have believed, and am convinced that He is able to guard what I have entrusted to Him for that day."

In all things and in all circumstances, in joy or in pain, as we walk in obedience to God, He works for our ultimate good. Job was a member of the "tested and tried" club; he ended up being better off after "the storm." When "Hurricane Satan" touched down and slammed through his home and business, inflicting his skin with bubonic boils, and whilst he was still in dire distress, Job reiterated his trust in God by saying, "*I know* that my Redeemer lives" (Job 19:25).

After God had seen Joseph through his seemingly endless troubles, Joseph, devoid of any bitterness and vengeance, was able to look straight into the eyes of his former tormentors (his own brothers) and say, "Do not be angry with yourselves for selling me here, because it was to save lives that God sent me ahead of you" (Genesis 45:5). In all things, God works; in all circumstances, let us thank Him. God is the master strategist, the great sculptor, the great potter; in all things, He'll work it out for your ultimate good. Thank Him; trust Him.

Prayer

I thank You, Lord, for where You have brought me from and where You have brought me to. I thank You, Lord, for where You are taking me next on this life journey. In all things great and small, in pain and in joy, I say, "Thank You," knowing that You are working it all out for my good.

Suggested Scriptures for Further Meditation

Jeremiah 29:11–12   Psalm 66:12   2 Corinthians 4:16–18

CHAPTER 51

THE INVINCIBLE, UNCONTAINABLE POWER OF RESURRECTION

The angel said to the women, "Do not be afraid, for I know that you are looking for Jesus, who was crucified. He is not here; he has risen, just as he said. Come and see the place where he lay. Then go quickly and tell his disciples: 'He has risen from the dead and is going ahead of you into Galilee. There you will see him.' Now I have told you."

—Matthew 28:5–7

Confusion rocked Satan's kingdom when news broke out by mid-morning on the third day that the Son of God had actually risen from the dead. Satan's spin doctors, operating through the chief priests, made every effort to keep the news from reaching the public domain. A hurriedly arranged press conference addressed by Satan's chief press secretary to deny the resurrection story (Matthew 28:11–15) was thrown into chaos when Mary Magdalene appeared on the scene to give a detailed account of her encounter with, firstly, an angel of the Lord who had told her that Jesus was risen, and secondly, with the resurrected Jesus Christ Himself who had told her to go tell the disciples that He had risen from the dead (Matthew 28:7–10).

Later in the day (Resurrection Sunday), details emerged about what had happened in Satan's kingdom from the time Jesus was buried on Good Friday through to the moment when He was raised from the dead by the power of the Holy Spirit. Satan himself could not be reached for immediate comment. Having been disarmed and stripped of his power by Jesus, who had made a public display of him and all his evil forces, Satan was downcast, crestfallen, and dumbfounded. Hell had come to a standstill. Resurrection power had brought hell to its knees! By sunset on Resurrection Sunday, Satan, defeated and deflated, issued his first public statement since Jesus' glorious resurrection from the dead. The statement read, "The head of Satan's security service and officers in charge of special operations whose responsibilities were to guard Jesus' tomb to prevent His resurrection have been summarily dismissed for gross negligence of duty" (see Matthew 27:62–66). This statement sent panic among the rest of the demons, as they feared losing their jobs as well.

On the other side, however, that is, in the camp of Jesus' disciples, there was ecstatic celebration over Jesus' resurrection. Having initially doubted Mary Magdalene's report of Jesus' resurrection, Peter and John ran to the tomb to verify it. But later in the evening of Resurrection Sunday, whilst the disciples met behind closed doors, Jesus appeared among them and said, "Peace to you" (John 20:19)! Case settled! Jesus said it, and He did it: "After three days, I will rise" (Matthew 27:63).

It's been over two thousand years since these events took place. The invincible, uncontainable power of the resurrection lives on, transforming lives and working in the lives of all who confess with their own lips that Jesus is Lord and believe in their hearts that God raised Him from the dead (Romans 10:9). This is the bedrock of the Christian faith and the power that enables us to triumph daily over Satan and sin (Ephesians 1:19–20; Romans 8:11). It is by this power of the resurrection that we are able to trample over serpents and scorpions. When we walk by way of the invincible power of the resurrection, we are unbeatable, unconquerable, unshakable, and indomitable. The uncontainable power of the resurrection is overwhelming, overpowering, and compelling. It subdues underfoot any opposition from hell.

The church (the body of believers) marches on and can sustain its forward march from victory to victory *only* by means of the power of the resurrection. When the apostle Paul first met with the Epicurean and Stoic philosophers in Athens (Acts 17:16–33), he achieved very little in terms of winning them to Christ because he engaged them intellectually and philosophically. We cannot win over people in our world today by using the power of oration and intellect. Having learned this hard lesson, the apostle Paul shifted gears, from the intellectual mode to the resurrection-power mode, when he journeyed to Corinth, a city of intellectuals notoriously noted for pursuing lustful pleasures. Paul wrote, "I came to you in weakness with great fear and trembling. My message and my preaching were not with wise and persuasive words, but with a demonstration of the Spirit's power" (1 Corinthians 2:3–4).

When resurrection power is at work in a believer or in a church, it is self-evident. When the sceptics in the days of Peter questioned the authority by which Peter and John healed the cripple at the Beautiful Gate (Acts 3:1–9), Peter told them that it was by the power in the name of Jesus, whom the sceptics crucified but who was raised by God from the dead. When the sceptics (Pharisees and Sadducees) threatened Peter and John and warned them not to preach about Jesus and the resurrection, the two disciples responded with an apostolic boldness and unfettered eloquence fueled by resurrection power (Acts 4:1–8,13–14). The sceptics were subdued; the church marched on, unbeatable, unconquerable, and unshakable.

By what authority and power are we living and operating as Christians these days?

Prayer

O Lord God, I pray You to breathe afresh upon the church the power of the resurrection so that the church enforces victory over the kingdom of darkness and establishes here on earth Your kingdom in the hearts of the inhabitants of this planet.

Suggested Scriptures for Further Meditation

1 Corinthians 15:17–19   Philippians 3:10   Colossians 2:15

CHAPTER 52

PROVING OURSELVES WORTHY

> At the end of the time set by the king to bring
> them in, the chief official presented them to
> Nebuchadnezzar. The king talked with them, and
> he found none equal to Daniel, Hananiah, Mishael
> and Azariah; so they entered the king's service. In
> every matter of wisdom and understanding about
> which the king questioned them, he found them ten
> times better than all the magicians and enchanters
> in his whole kingdom.
>
> —Daniel 1:18–20

Daniel is one of my most favourite personalities in the Bible.
Unlike other characters in the Bible, such as Jacob, Moses,
and Samuel, whose life stories were recorded right from birth,
Daniel's life came into focus when he was in his teens, probably
the age of fifteen. He was among a group of Jewish children who
were taken away to Babylon when Nebuchadnezzar conquered
Jerusalem. Daniel was chosen based on selection criteria defined
by King Nebuchadnezzar, who wanted children of Israel, children
of the royal family, children in whom there was no blemish but

who were well favoured, and skilful in all wisdom, cunning in knowledge, and understanding in science, and who had the ability within them to stand in the king's palace (Daniel 1:3–4).

Away from home, from parents, relatives, and friends, Daniel found himself in a foreign land with a different culture, religion, language, norms, values, traditions, education, and political system. Every effort was made by King Nebuchadnezzar and the state of Babylon to make Daniel and his co-captives think, act, and behave like Babylonians and, above all, to serve the king and the purposes of the kingdom of Babylon. But there was something in the inside of Daniel and his three colleagues, namely, Shadrach, Meshach, and Abednego, that Babylon could not change. Babylon could not change the allegiance and the reverence that Daniel, Shadrach, Meshach, and Abednego had for the God of Israel, or their commitment to the commandments and statutes they were taught by the Jewish religious system.

In many respects, we believers in Christ Jesus share a similar background with Daniel. The apostle Peter makes it irrevocably clear that we are a chosen generation of a royal ancestry and that we are peculiar (1 Peter 2:9). Because of the redemptive work of the blood of Jesus, we are without blemish, we are highly favoured by grace, and we have the mind of Christ and therefore have discernment and knowledge girded with wisdom. Christ has given us the means to stand before God, our King. Like Daniel, we live in a world (kingdom) whose systems of belief, practice, and behaviour are contrary to ours. It is a world that desires to change us; it is a world that wants us to think, act, and behave like it does. But we are of Christ; we love God and we live by the teachings of God's Word. Our world today is like Babylon in the days of Daniel. Even though Daniel lived in Babylon, he was not of Babylon. Even though we live in this world, we are not of this world (John 17:16).

Daniel purposed in his heart not to think, act, or behave like Babylonians, even though there was much pressure on him to conform to the tenets of Babylon. He requested the prince of the eunuchs in the palace of King Nebuchadnezzar not to force him to eat and drink the Babylonian way, but to allow him, Shadrach, Meshach, and Abednego to eat and drink the Jewish way. It was a matter of choice between the Babylonian way (lifestyle) and the Jewish way (lifestyle). Jesus Christ, in His days on earth, did make mention of two ways: the narrow way and the broad way. To help people make the right choice, Jesus told the audience in His day, "I am the Way, the Truth and the Life" (John 14:6).

Every choice we make in this life is or will be tested in the course of time. And so Daniel's choice and the choice of the other three were tested. The outcomes were crystal clear after a period of time: the countenances of Daniel and his colleagues appeared fairer and fatter in flesh than those of all the children who did eat a portion of the king's meat (the Babylonian way). A life lived in honour of God is always rewarded by God. When the children of both ways were finally evaluated by King Nebuchadnezzar, the king found Daniel, Shadrach, Meshach, and Abednego ten times better than all the magicians and astrologers in his kingdom. Daniel and his friends continued to prove and demonstrate the worthiness of the choice they made to live according to God's way. Time after time, Babylon could not subdue them or change them; rather, Babylon began to acknowledge the God of Daniel.

Babylon and its king, Nebuchadnezzar, realized that the Spirit that was in Daniel was greater than the spirit that was behind Babylonian systems, beliefs, and practices.

Daniel was a type of "church" in Babylon. He was both light and salt to Babylon. He proved his worthiness by his lifestyle and the anointing that was upon him during his entire life in Babylon. Daniel demonstrated that when light shines in darkness, darkness surrenders. Babylon could not change Daniel; Daniel changed Babylon. As Christians, are we changing our world today, or is the world changing us? Are we by our lifestyles proving to the world that the choice we have made in honour of God and in obedience to our Lord and Saviour Jesus Christ is worthy? Daniel and his colleagues, though they were in Babylon, proved by their faith in God that they were not of Babylon. Even though we (believers in Christ) are in this world, we are not of this world (John 17:14–16).

Prayer

Lord, I want to live above the world, not conforming to the world's systems of belief and practice, which are at variance with Your revealed will as contained in the Bible and as inspired by the Holy Spirit. Help me to reign in this life, with You upholding the tenets of the faith, righteousness, and love as revealed in You and by You. Thank You, Lord, for the fact that although I am in this world, I am not of this world.

Suggested Scriptures for Further Meditation

1 Corinthians 6:20   Colossians 1:10   Ephesians 4:1

ABOUT THE AUTHOR

Rev. Jonathan Yaw Martey is a gifted preacher and teacher of the Word of God. A pharmacist by profession, he is the senior pastor of Spirit and Word Church in Accra, Ghana. Rev. Martey is married to a lovely gifted preacher, Rev. Josephine Martey. They have seven children.

Printed in the United States
By Bookmasters